The Mountain Bike Guide

to *Summit County, Colorado*

*47 Backcountry Rides Around
Copper Mountain, Breckenridge, Montezuma, Keystone,
Vail Pass, Frisco, Dillon and the Lower Blue River Valley*

by Laura Rossetter

Sage Creek Press
Silverthorne, Colorado

Book design-Johnson Printing
Cover design-Anita Koverman
Author photo-Todd Powell
All other photos-Laura/Steve Rossetter
Printing-Johnson Printing

Although every effort has been made to ensure that the information in this guide is accurate; conditions do change. It is strongly recommended that you consult with local bike shops or the U.S. Forest Service about specific safety and condition situations before riding. Nowhere should you assume that this guide is encouraging or recommending you attempt something or ride a specific route. Mountain biking is a challenging sport containing potential for personal injury. In the outdoors, hazards (both natural and man-made) can present themselves at any time. The author cannot be held responsible for any changes in road or trail conditions since the time of printing or for injuries resulting from any ride selected in this book. Ride at your own risk!

ISBN 0-9621978-1-5

Revised and expanded second edition, 1993

Sage Creek Press
PO Box 1373
Silverthorne, Colorado 80498

CONTENTS

RIDES AROUND FRISCO

RIDES AROUND COPPER MOUNTAIN-VAIL PASS

RIDES AROUND THE LOWER BLUE RIVER VALLEY

APPENDIX

ACKNOWLEDGEMENTS

During the process of writing this book, I was aided by many individuals and businesses who gave their time, advice and support. My heartfelt gratitude goes to all of these generous people and especially to the following:

Tom Healy and Mark Traum of the U.S. Forest Service, Dillon Ranger District, for providing valuable information as well as their support and approval; the folks at Mountain Cyclery and Ski whose positive attitude and practical advice helped motivate me; Dave Randall of Summit County Velo Bike Club whose knowledge about local terrain proved invaluable; Doug of CanAmerican Graphics, who provided technical assistance on the computer and expertise in the design and layout of this book; Steve Cottrell for his professional advice and printing services; Anita Koverman for the cover illustration; Alpenrose Press for sharing their knowledge of publishing procedures; Lars Anderson, who patiently answered my numerous computer related questions; all of the tireless proofreaders who spent so much time on the manuscript; and the many mountain bikers who generously shared their knowledge about riding conditions and provided companionship as my riding partners. A special thanks to my favorite biking buddy, Steve, for his willingness to explore, useful advice and continual support.

While researching the second edition, I was aided by Sue Miller, (who was a huge help!), Sue McHenry and Jeff Bailey of the U.S. Forest Service; Mike Zobbe of the Breckenridge Fat Tire Society and Ellen Hollinshead, who both provided valuable information on route locations; Dan Vaughn and several other Keystone employees who discussed trail systems in their area; Bill Stoehr for generously providing Trails Illustrated maps; Scott Hobson, who answered many questions on land access; Alex Chappell for addressing wildlife concerns; Sara Ballantyne, David Nelson, Portia Masterson, Stuart MacDonald, and Jim Hasenauer for their kind words; Todd Powell for shooting the author photo and Johnson Printing for their design and printing services. Proofreaders again receive my appreciation for their much needed assistance. Thanks also to the many riding companions (especially my father), who willingly followed me through new terrain. Once again the completion of this book is due to the support of my husband, Steve, whose cheerfulness, energy and patience have kept me going on many biking expeditions.

Summit County, Colorado, simply put, is a mountain biker's mecca. Its location deep within the Rocky Mountains guarantees spectacular terrain brimming with hundreds of miles of backcountry roads and trails. The region, easily accessed by driving 75 miles west of Denver on Interstate 70, offers the unique combination of a fascinating mining heritage and surroundings dominated by snow-capped peaks. Bikers of all abilities will enjoy a seemingly endless variety of riding options ranging from a gentle climb on a deserted railroad grade to a challenging single track ascent along windswept ridges of the Continental Divide. The richly varied topography of Summit County presents backcountry bikers with many choices: following historic byways past aging mining camps, retracing the abandoned routes of railroads that once passed through the county and investigating the many high alpine roads and trails crisscrossing innumerable sky-piercing peaks. *The Mountain Bike Guide to Summit County, Colorado* is an invitation for you to explore, from the seat of a mountain bike, the vast network of dirt roads and trails that make Summit County the perfect playground for fat tire enthusiasts of all abilities.

Backcountry Bicycling Tips

Rules and Regulations

Summit County is receiving increasing use by recreationalists. Mountain bikers, as a relatively new addition to the list of backcountry users, are under a lot of scrutiny. Responsibility is the key word in keeping attitudes toward off-road cyclists on a positive level. Mountain bikers venturing into the backcountry should be equipped with the basic knowledge to be responsible for their own actions and safety and for the environment in which they ride.

Conflicts with hikers, horsemen, motorized vehicles and other bikers are easily avoided by following a few simple but important rules concerning mountain biker's trail etiquette. Adherence to these rules is vital in promoting responsible backcountry biking.

HIKERS: Yield the right of way to hikers. Make enough noise to avoid surprising hikers and when approaching from behind, make your presence known well in advance, then inform them of your desire to pass.

HORSEBACK RIDERS: Horses are easily spooked by bicycles. When encountering riders, dismount and leave the trail on the downhill side so they can continue. Pass horses only after telling the riders of your intentions and allowing them to bring their horses under control.

MOUNTAIN BIKERS: Downhill riders yield to uphill riders. When overtaking another bike, communicate your intention and choose an area that provides enough space for passing. Yield the trail to bikers wishing to pass you.

VEHICLES: Jeeps, motorbikes and all-terrain vehicles are common in Summit County and share some routes with mountain bikes. If you encounter a vehicle allow it plenty of room to pass. You'll find that mountain bikes are often faster than vehicles on descents. When passing, be aware that they usually have no idea you're near.

In addition to awareness of other trail users, it's important to take precautions that help preserve the natural surroundings. Adopt the "soft cycling" approach toward backcountry biking, which means minimizing your impact on the environment. Be sensitive toward your surroundings and keep in mind a few important tips.

1. Stay on designated roads and trails to protect surrounding soil and vegetation. Refrain from riding through mud holes, bogs, etc., which could leave long-lasting ruts. Minimize potential erosion by not shortcutting switchbacks. Since many backcountry routes receive little maintenance it is the rider's responsibility to ensure that no environmental damage occurs. Avoid riding over vegetation, especially above timberline, where plant life is extremely fragile.

2. Ride in control. Check your speed and be ready to stop safely at any instance. Avoid locking your brakes, which causes unnecessary trail damage.

3. Avoid spooking wildlife. Animals are easily frightened by an unannounced approach. Forewarning animals (by creating noise or attaching a bell to your bike and stopping immediately when you see them) **BEFORE** you startle them gives them a choice in how to avoid or observe you. Remember, you are a visitor in *their* home.

4. Running livestock is a serious offense. If you encounter cattle, stop or ride by them slowly so they have time to respond without panicking.

5. Wilderness areas are closed to mountain bikes. This includes Eagle's Nest Wilderness Area, which encompasses most of the Gore Range.

6. Respect private property. Summit County has a lot of it. Some of the trails ridden most frequently are not in this guide because they're actually on private land. Many of the described routes pass by mining remains that are also on private property. Please don't disturb these sites. They are easily viewed from the road or trail. Some of the trailhead access directions and rides follow public access routes through private lands. It is critical that you remain on the designated route in these situations. As new access roads and residential developments appear in Summit County, several bike routes have been or will be closed or re-routed. Please use the provided alternates and respect all "No Trespassing" signs. If you feel a trail has been wrongly closed, contact the appropriate county or Forest Service authority. Expect continual change in backcountry access routes as the county's rapid growth continues and deal with it in a positive, flexible manner. Don't push your luck; many landowners have no sympathy for trespassers and any lack of respect gives all mountain bikers a bad name.

7. Leave gates as you found them or as marked.

8. Protect Summit County's mining heritage by helping to preserve the historic structures encountered on many of the rides.

All of these guidelines are easily implemented. Responsible biking techniques, courtesy on the trail and sensitivity toward the environment help promote a positive public attitude toward mountain bikers and their use of the backcountry.

Preparations and Precautions

When riding in the backcountry you must be self-sufficient. Know your limitations, carry the necessary supplies and be prepared to handle any situation that might arise.

Equipping yourself properly for a backcountry ride means always bringing a few essential items that can be strapped under your seat in a small bag, carried in a daypack, in a fanny pack or on a rack. These necessities include:

- **TIRE IRONS**
- **SPARE TUBE**
- **TUBE PATCH KIT**
- **PUMP**
- **MAP**
- **COMPASS**
- **POCKET KNIFE**
- **LIQUIDS**
- **HIGH ENERGY SNACKS**
- **SUNSCREEN**
- **SUNGLASSES**
- **CLOTHING FOR INCLEMENT WEATHER**

Additional tools and accessories to consider are:

- **4–5–6 mm ALLEN WRENCHES**
- **6" CRESCENT WRENCH**
- **8–9–10 mm WRENCHES**
- **1" STRAPPING TAPE FOR TIRE RIPS**
- **SMALL FLAT- AND PHILLIPS-HEAD SCREWDRIVERS**
- **MATCHES**
- **FIRST AID KIT**
- **CHAIN LUBRICANT**
- **CHAIN TOOL**

A word on mountain biking attire; comfort is important. Bike in clothing that works for you and bring enough layers to remain comfortable in changing weather conditions. Wear a helmet every time you ride. Even if you never plan to do any aggressive biking, a helmet should be a mandatory piece of your biking equipment.

Having the appropriate supplies is only the first step toward being prepared for a backcountry ride. Your safety in the mountains means planning a ride carefully. Choose a route within your capabilities. Keep in mind your physical condition, ability to adapt to high altitudes and expertise on a mountain bike. Don't hesitate to try out a variety of terrain but be sensible about when you've reached your limits. Mountain biking can be a very demanding activity, especially in Colorado, where most of the rides are at elevations between 8,000 and 12,000 feet.

If you're unfamiliar with the area you've chosen to ride in, carry the suggested map for that ride. Always leave word with someone about your destination. A word of caution about riding around Summit County's mining regions: a lot of open mine shafts, pits and unstable structures dot the terrain. Do not explore, inspect or get near any mining operations or old buildings. Not only are you probably trespassing, but are also putting yourself in potentially dangerous situations.

Before riding make sure your bike is in good functioning condition to avoid needless mechanical problems while on the trail. This relates to rental bikes also. If you're renting, go for a quick spin on the bike to make sure everything is operating correctly before taking off on a ride.

Take care of yourself during the ride. Drink plenty of liquids. Wear sunscreen to shield your skin from the intense, high-altitude sun. Protect yourself during hunting season by wearing bright colors and being exceptionally cautious when pedaling on less-used routes. If the route takes you above timberline, start early and carry adequate clothing for those infamous Colorado mountain storms that can catch you when you least expect it. Remember that rain can suddenly change route conditions. A previously passive trail can turn into a technical challenge after a torrential downpour.

Being prepared with the proper equipment and using common sense when planning for and during rides should provide you with an exciting, enjoyable backcountry experience.

How to Use This Guide

The ride descriptions in this guide follow a set format. An information capsule gives a brief overview of each ride, listing important features that tell you at a glance if the ride is appropriate for your ability. Detailed narrative is provided for the access, description, options and comments sections. Below are brief explanations of these features.

DISTANCE: Approximate round-trip mileage is given for each ride. A cyclometer was used to record mileage, making the distances fairly accurate. Mileage is mentioned occasionally in the ride description (in **bold** and usually in parentheses) and is often marked on the corresponding map. It helps when navigating to have an idea of the distance you've covered and mileages are often given in reference to a distinct landmark or trail junction.

TIME: The estimated time is geared for the average rider and accounts for the hours needed, including short breaks, to complete a ride. Time varies greatly depending on rider's ability and his or her goals. You can determine if you fit within the given times or are consistently faster or slower after riding a couple of the described routes.

RATING: Rating a backcountry road or trail for rideability is a challenging task. Varied levels of competence and fitness make each mountain biker approach a route from a different perspective. Consequently, the ride ratings provide only a general idea of the difficulty of each ride. This difficulty level indicates what overall technical and physical abilities are needed to complete a ride. Ratings are based on the rideability of the road or trail and take into account obstacles such as loose rock, roots and stream crossings. Also considered are the length of the ride, elevation gain and loss and steepness of climbs (gradient).

EASY: Minimal biking experience and physical exertion are required. Routes contain very few technical obstacles. Climbs and descents are gradual. However, for someone not used to exercising at elevations above 8,000 feet, there are very few truly "easy" rides in Summit County. If you fit into this category and aren't acclimated to higher elevations, you can still have a great backcountry biking experience. Just be prepared to take a little longer, rest more frequently and maybe do some walking.

MODERATE: Requires a moderate level of physical effort. Some long, gradual or short, steep climbs occur. You must be capable of maneuvering your bike over some obstacles such as loose rocks or small stream crossings. Walking your bike for short distances may be necessary.

9

MORE DIFFICULT: Good physical condition is necessary for riding up extended steep grades. Elevation gains can be considerable. You should have solid mountain biking skills and the technical ability to negotiate rocks, streams, bogs, ruts, etc. Some walking is likely.

ADVANCED: You need to be able to ride for extended periods over rough terrain. Routes require expert riding skills. Long climbs and extensive elevation gains demand top physical condition. Occasional hazardous route conditions require periods of walking.

Many ride ratings are a combination of two categories, for example, moderate-more difficult. Sometimes a ride starts out easy and progresses to an advanced rating or it may be almost entirely moderate with one small section of advanced climbing in the middle. If a ride fits into this situation, an asterisk marks the rating that describes the majority of the ride, for example, easy*-more difficult. An explanation of the asterisk is provided in the "comments" section. Also, the ride description will elaborate on situations (usually a significant terrain change) that necessitate a different rating.

The ratings give you an idea of what to expect. You make your own decisions on what to attempt, using the rating only as a tool to help find a ride compatible with your ability. Read the entire description and experiment. Don't let longer distances scare you. Some of the longer rides have an easier rating due to a less strenuous level of rideability. Some short rides have more difficult ratings because of technical, strenuous riding. In addition, ratings only apply when taking the described trail direction. Following the direction opposite the describe route may alter the rating. Ratings are based on current road and trail conditions which often change due to weather or man-made causes.

ELEVATION, GAIN: The lowest and highest elevations are given for each ride. The gain gives the change in elevation between the highest and lowest point. This *net* elevation gain can be deceiving since many rides ascend and descend several times.

TYPE: Each ride is classified either as a loop (riding in one direction with little or no backtracking) or as an out and back (riding out in one direction and backtracking on the same route). Also included in this section is the ride's categorization as a dirt road, trail, bike path (paved) or paved road. Most rides are a combination of these categories with paved roads being used only when necessary to access a route or complete a loop.

SEASON: The suggested time of the year gives you a general idea of when you can do a ride. Summit County's fickle weather makes it tough to predict exactly when mountain bike season starts and ends. Snowstorms in May and June or sunny, dry weather in November can shorten or lengthen the biking season considerably. Generally, routes above 10,500 feet won't be bikeable until late May. Above 11,000 feet, biking season starts in June with snowdrifts at even higher elevations and on northern exposures well into July. Remember, riding a road or trail too early in the season can destroy it for the entire summer. Waiting for routes to dry completely after spring runoff pays off with better riding conditions for the remainder of the season.

MAPS: USGS 7.5 Series topographic (USGS 7.5) and Trails Illustrated (TI) maps are listed for the area covering each ride. The two types vary in the information they provide and date of currency. Although the 7.5 Series are the most detailed, the Trails Illustrated are the most recently updated. I personally use Trails Illustrated maps whenever possible. Qualities including waterproofness, durability, detail, a symbol identifying bikeable routes and continual revisions make these maps excellent tools for mountain bikers.

The map included with each ride description is a portion of the USGS County Series 1:50,000. This series covers a large area and reduces well into book form. But many have not been updated recently and some of the side roads and trails mentioned in the descriptions are not shown on these maps. A list of the County Series maps I used is shown in the "maps" section of the appendix. The Forest Service maps covering Summit County are also listed in the appendix.

Remember, some routes shown on the topo maps will not correspond to what is actually in the backcountry. It's to your advantage to have some navigating ability, to be able to distinguish landmarks and elevation changes and to know how to use these skills when reading a map. I strongly advise carrying a complete map of the region to supplement what the book provides.

Shown below are symbols used on the topographic maps:

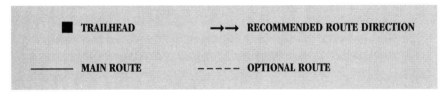

■ TRAILHEAD   **→→ RECOMMENDED ROUTE DIRECTION**

———— **MAIN ROUTE**   – – – – – **OPTIONAL ROUTE**

HILL PROFILE: This graph combines elevation and distance statistics to give you an idea of the amount of ascending and descending within a ride. It shows whether elevation is gained or lost all at once or in series of ups and downs. A topo map with 80-foot contours was used to develop the graph. Minor elevation changes of less than 80 feet aren't shown. There are 12 profiles whose mileage increments deviate from the standard.

ACCESS: Access descriptions provide directions on how to get to the trailhead using mileage and landmarks. All access routes originate from Interstate-70 and can be driven in a passenger vehicle. The described rides require only one car, unless you choose the shuttle options mentioned for some rides. Remember: signs, landmarks, road numbers, etc. may change, making some of the directions less accurate. Also, please park well off any roadway and away from private property or driveways.

DESCRIPTION: Detailed descriptions are given for each ride. I used landmarks and directions such as "right turn" or "left turn" as navigational aids. In addition, variations in terrain, side roads, trails and distinctive natural features are mentioned to help you follow a route. Terminology frequently used includes *cairn*, which is a pile of rocks used to mark a route. Read the entire description before attempting a ride. Details such as difficulty of climbs, traffic encountered and when a ride changes from one rating to another are discussed. Of course, situations different from the described route are a possibility. Trail re-routings, washouts, road closures or missing signs (a common occurrence in Summit County) may hinder your ability to navigate. Road numbers, particularly Forest Service roads, change frequently and may not correspond to the route numbers mentioned in the description. Because of rampant growth in Summit County you should anticipate numerous changes from the ride description in details such as: additions of new roads and trails, closures and re-routings, pavement on roads which were previously dirt and encroaching residential development into backcountry areas.

OPTIONS: This section suggests additional or alternate routes branching off the main ride. An option can be used to add more miles to the described route or taken as a completely separate ride. Optional routes are identified on the maps by a dashed line.

COMMENTS: Specifics on terrain changes pertaining to the ride rating are highlighted here. In addition, anything of particular importance or uniqueness, such as traffic, exposure above timberline and private property is detailed in this section.

Please use this guidebook only as a general reference on where to ride. All directions were accurate when the routes were last visited but changes do occur. I strongly recommend that you consult with local bike shops or the Forest Service about specific safety and route condition considerations before you go riding. Finally, do not use this guide as a substitute for your own good judgement. Take responsibility for making decisions about preparing adequately for a ride and choose routes within your ability. Most important, once you feel you've shopped, fixed, packed, read and mapped yourself silly, go out there, hop on your bike and have the time of your life!

High alpine cruising on Georgia Pass.

Views from 12,498 ft. Ptarmigan Peak

Miner's cabin high above Peru Creek

RIDE 1   BLUE LAKES

DISTANCE: 7 miles
TIME: 1-2 hours
RATING: Easy*- moderate
ELEVATION: 10,840-11,680 ft.
GAIN: 840 ft.
TYPE: Out&back; dirt rd.
SEASON: Late June to early October
MAPS: USGS 7.5 Breckenridge
TI Breckenridge South

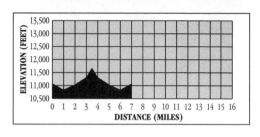

A short ride takes you quickly above timberline and offers breathtaking views of shimmering lakes and craggy peaks.

ACCESS: Drive 7.6 miles south of Breckenridge on HWY 9 toward Hoosier Pass. Turn right onto road #850 (Blue Lakes Road). Turn right shortly after onto road #851. Drive about a mile, looking for a jeep road forking left (marked with an arrow). Park in one of the several pulloffs on the right near this spur.

DESCRIPTION: Backtrack down road #851 until connecting with Blue Lakes Road. Turn right and climb gradually up the valley past some houses (respect the private property in this area), staying on road #850. As this route climbs higher it passes over some short, steep pitches. At a junction **(3.0 mi)** take the right fork, which swings around the right side of the lower lake. As you climb steadily toward the upper lake spectacular views unfold. Looking south you'll see the remains of several mines, including parts of a tramway, still clinging to the cliffs of North Star Mountain. The road ends at the top of the dam. At this point you are surrounded by some of Summit County's highest peaks. Quandary Peak, a "fourteener", looms on the right. Bald Mountain is the dominating peak when looking down and across the valley. An enjoyable hike takes off from the right side of the spillway and into a drainage north of upper Blue Lake. Return as you came.

OPTION: You can lengthen this ride by continuing on road #851 beyond your parking spot. It drops into McCullough Gulch, an equally striking mountain drainage. Several roads in this area offer short biking/hiking explorations.

COMMENTS: *Although short, this ride can be physically demanding due to its high altitude. Be prepared for continually changing weather conditions when riding above timberline. Expect traffic, mainly on weekends.

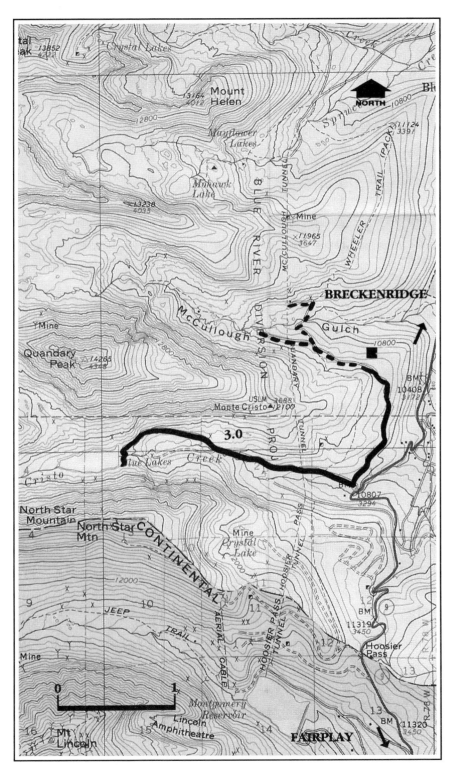

RIDE 2   BOREAS PASS

DISTANCE: 12.5 miles

TIME: 2-3 hours

RATING: Easy

ELEVATION: 10,360-11,481 ft.

GAIN: 1,121 ft.

TYPE: Out&back; dirt rd.

SEASON: Mid-June to mid-October

MAPS: USGS 7.5 Breckenridge-Boreas Pass
TI Breckenridge South

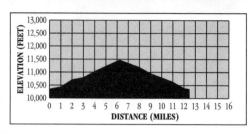

Boreas Pass Road follows an old railroad grade from Breckenridge to the Continental Divide. Remains of the nation's highest post office and a narrow-gauge depot are perched on top of the pass.

ACCESS: Drive through Breckenridge on HWY 9. Turn left beyond the stoplight on the south end of town onto Boreas Pass Road. Drive 3.5 miles up this winding road to pavement's end. Park in a pulloff on the left where the road becomes dirt.

DESCRIPTION: Begin climbing toward Boreas Pass. The ride follows a railroad grade which was originally the route of the Denver, South Park and Pacific Railroad. This well maintained dirt road climbs gradually through beautiful aspen groves, making it a superb autumn ride. Pass Baker's Tank, which stored water for railway use **(3.0 mi)**. Continue climbing along the flank of Bald Mountain. Increasingly spectacular views unfold as you near timberline. Reach Boreas Pass and the Continental Divide **(6.3 mi)**. There's plenty of exploring to be done on roads branching off through meadows carpeted with wildflowers. To the left are remains of buildings that once housed the depot and post office. The road continues down to the vast expanse of South Park and into the town of Como. (See option 2.) From the pass, return as you came.

OPTION 1: Novice bikers can leave a shuttle vehicle at the trailhead, drive to the pass and ride only the descent.

OPTION 2: The ride into Como remains easy but tacks an additional 11 miles (one-way) to the trip.

COMMENTS: Numerous side trails and roads branch off this route. Try rides 3 and 10 for additional exploring in the area. Expect traffic, especially on weekends. A portion of the ride is above timberline; plan accordingly.

The Ten Mile Range fills the western skyline from Boreas Pass Road.

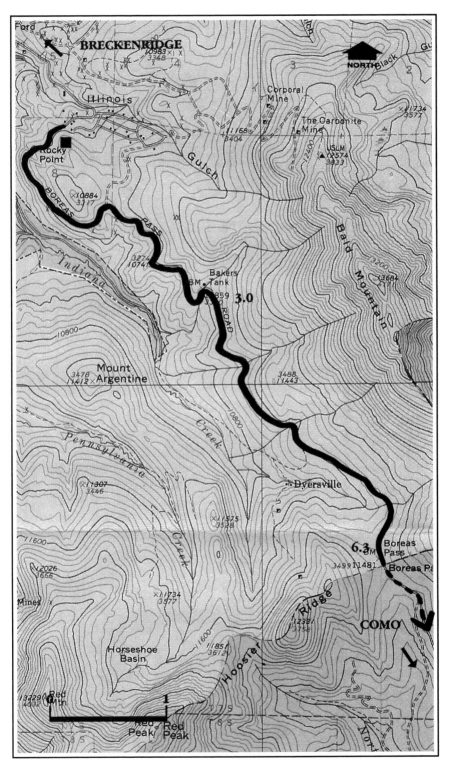

RIDE 3   BAKER'S TANK LOOP

DISTANCE: 5.5 miles
TIME: 1-2 hours
RATING: Moderate
ELEVATION: 10,360-10,850 ft.
GAIN: 490 ft.
TYPE: Loop; trail/dirt rd.
SEASON: Mid-June to mid-October
MAPS: USGS 7.5 Breckenridge-Boreas Pass
TI Breckenridge South

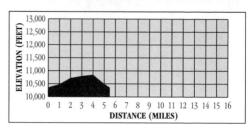

An easy climb up the gradual pitch of Boreas Pass Road takes you to a hidden-away single track full of high speed cruising.

ACCESS: Drive through Breckenridge on HWY 9. Turn left beyond the stoplight on the south end of town onto Boreas Pass Road. Drive 3.5 miles up this winding road to pavement's end. Park in a pulloff on the left where the road becomes dirt.

DESCRIPTION: Climb gradually along the well maintained Boreas Pass Road to Baker's Tank **(3.0 mi)**. Used to store water for the Denver, South Park and Pacific railway, the original tank held 9,305 gallons of water. The current structure is actually a restored replacement of the original Baker's Tank. Turn onto the side road forking left before the tank. (See ride 2 to continue toward the pass.) Take another left almost immediately and climb steeply to a single track. Veer left and pedal along this nearly level trail as it winds around the left side of a hill, clinging to edge of a steep slope. Curve right, meander along a forested hillside and encounter a 3-way junction **(4.0 mi)**. Take the left fork (although the right fork looks tempting it leads to private property) which dives down a wooded slope. Using tightly spaced trees as slalom gates, this descent twists and turns just enough to keep you from reaching warp speed. Connect with an old road **(4.6 mi)**. Turn left (once again a right turn leads to private land) and follow the road for a very short distance as it curves left. As the road straightens and descends, look for a faint single track forking right. (It might take a couple of minutes of patient searching to find and follow the first segment.) The trail veers right through a couple of campsites before curving left into the trees where it becomes more visible. The final descent starts out smooth, then drops more steeply over a rock-filled path. Pass a couple of side trails on the left and drop onto Boreas Pass Road **(5.4 mi)**. Turn right and pedal around the corner to your vehicle.

OPTION: If you found the first section of trail extremely challenging and want to avoid the second half, stay on the dirt road. It connects with Boreas Pass Road which you can follow back down to your vehicle.

COMMENTS: Expect traffic on Boreas Pass Road which is bordered by aspen groves, making it a spectacular fall ride. Avoid the single track after heavy rainfall.

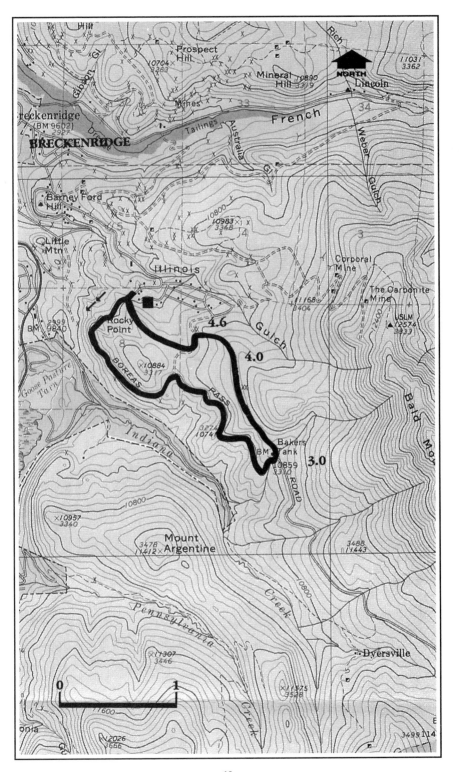

RIDE 4   BOREAS PASS LOOP

DISTANCE: 26 miles
TIME: 4-5 hours
RATING: Moderate*
ELEVATION: 10,096-11,481 ft.
GAIN: 1,385 ft.
TYPE: Out&back/loop; dirt rd.
SEASON: Mid-June to mid-October
MAPS: USGS 7.5 Breckenridge-Boreas Pass-Como
TI Breckenridge South

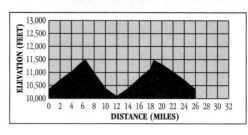

Highlights of this pleasant cruise include a complete tour of the Boreas Pass section of the Denver, South Park & Pacific railroad grade and a side trip down an abandoned wagon route.

ACCESS: Drive through Breckenridge on HWY 9. Turn left beyond the stoplight on the south end of town onto Boreas Pass Road. Drive 3.5 miles up this winding road to pavement's end. Park in a pulloff on the left where the road becomes dirt.

DESCRIPTION: Climb gradually up this smooth dirt road to Boreas Pass (**6.3 mi**). Continue from the top as the road drops toward South Park. Descend a short distance to the first curve (about .5 miles) and look for a faint double track dropping off the right side of the road into the trees. An orange diamond attached to a tree marks this route. Follow this abandoned road, once the wagon route from South Park to the pass. Called the "Gold Dust Trail", it drops more steeply than the railroad grade and contains several technical sections of loose rock and stream crossings. Connect with a well-traveled dirt road (**8.5 mi**). Turn left and enjoy a smoother descent along the valley's edge. Reach a 3-way junction near Selkirk Campground (**10 mi**). (The described route continues straight; see option 1 for a shortcut using the left fork.) After fording a stream continue descending, now along the edge of private property. At the next major junction turn left onto a graded county road and descend a bit further to a fork on the left for Boreas Pass Road (**12.3 mi**). (Continuing straight here would take you another 3.5 miles to the historic community of Como.) It's climbing time again as you turn left and follow the railroad grade around a knoll, through dense aspen groves and past Davis Overlook which provides expansive views toward the southern horizon. Formidable peaks along the Continental Divide create a scenic diversion as you pedal gradually upward. Pass the Selkirk Campground shortcut (**15.6 mi**) and continue climbing until crossing the pass again (**19.5 mi**). A final descent along now-familiar terrain brings you quickly to your vehicle.

OPTION: To eliminate 4.3 miles from the total distance, turn left at the junction by Selkirk Campground and ascend on a 1.3-mile shortcut to Boreas Pass Road.

COMMENTS: *Boreas Pass Road is an easy pedal but some technical skill is needed to negotiate several rough and rocky areas of the wagon road. A section of this ride is above timberline; plan accordingly. Expect traffic on Boreas Pass Road which is bordered by aspen groves, making it a great fall ride.

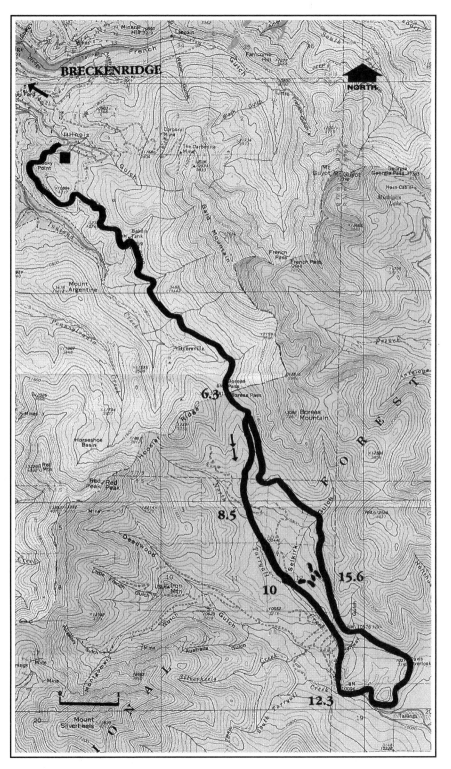

RIDE 5   BURRO TRAIL–SPRUCE CREEK

DISTANCE: 9.5 miles
TIME: 3 hours
RATING: Moderate-more difficult*
ELEVATION: 9,840-10,960 ft.
GAIN: 1,120 ft.
TYPE: Out&back/loop; dirt rd./trail
SEASON: Mid-June to early October
MAPS: USGS 7.5 Breckenridge
TI Breckenridge South

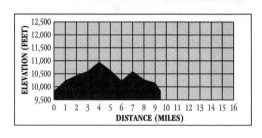

A combination of three separate trail systems that alternate between dirt road and trail explores the Spruce Creek drainage.

ACCESS: Drive through Breckenridge on HWY 9. Turn right at the stoplight at the south end of town onto South Park Avenue. Turn left onto Village Road and follow it to a parking lot on the left below Beaver Run Resort. Park near the ski slope and trailhead sign.

DESCRIPTION: Follow the ski area access road that leaves the parking lot and climbs Peak 9. Almost immediately, turn left onto the Burro Trail (marked by a sign). Cross a stream and follow the main trail which is marked by blue diamonds. Climb along the left side of the stream past many spurs to the left and right and over several technical sections. The trail veers away from the stream, meandering through the forest and passing more spurs. Climb to and connect with an abandoned road **(2.0 mi)**. Turn left onto the road, ride over an extremely rocky section and ascend gradually along the hillside. Cross the Crystal Lakes jeep road **(3.0 mi)**. Continue a short distance further on the trail until merging with Spruce Creek Road. Turn right and pedal up this road for almost a mile to a junction with another road and the Wheeler Trail. Continuing straight leads to Mayflower Lake, a right leads to Crystal Lakes (see options). For this ride turn left onto the Wheeler Trail and drop into the drainage. Ford three streams before intersecting the Spruce Creek Trail **(4.4 mi)**. Leave the Wheeler Trail (see ride 6 for its continuation) and turn left onto Spruce Creek Trail. It descends along the right side of this drainage over several tricky sections filled with roots and rocks. A couple of fallen trees and muddy areas require quick portages. The moderate gradient alternates with short, steep drops. After about a mile of descending, cross a couple of old ditches and Spruce Creek. Shortly after, at a 4-way intersection, cross an old road and continue descending on the trail. Below a steep rocky section you pass a fork to the right. Veer left and ride into the lower trailhead parking on Spruce Creek Road **(5.8 mi)**. Turn left and climb for .5 miles on the rocky but moderate pitch of the jeep road. Shortly after passing the Crystal Lakes spur look for the Burro Trail forking right. Turn onto the trail and descend along this now-familiar route back to your vehicle.

OPTIONS: From the junction of Spruce Creek Road and the Wheeler Trail advanced riders have a couple of options for exploring two high alpine drainages.

OPTION 1: To reach Mayflower Lake, nestled just below a rugged headwall in Spruce Creek drainage, continue climbing on Spruce Creek Road for another .1 miles. Fork right at a less used road marked by a sign for "jeep trail". A strenuous .7-mile climb over rocky terrain and challenging ledges on an abandoned road brings you to picturesque Mayflower Lake.

OPTION 2: To explore Crystal Lakes (the next drainage north) turn right from the junction onto a well maintained road. Climb for .7 miles along this road to its dead end at a concrete dam. Follow a trail from the other side of the dam to a jeep road. Turn left and climb steeply up this road for another 1.5 miles to a striking high alpine cirque, lower Crystal Lake and a collapsed cabin.

COMMENTS: *Although elevation gains are moderate, much of this ride is rocky and requires some technical skill. Many spurs along the Burro Trail, especially near the ski area, provide hours of additional exploring. Expect both hikers and horsemen on the trails (which get very muddy after heavy rain and should be avoided).

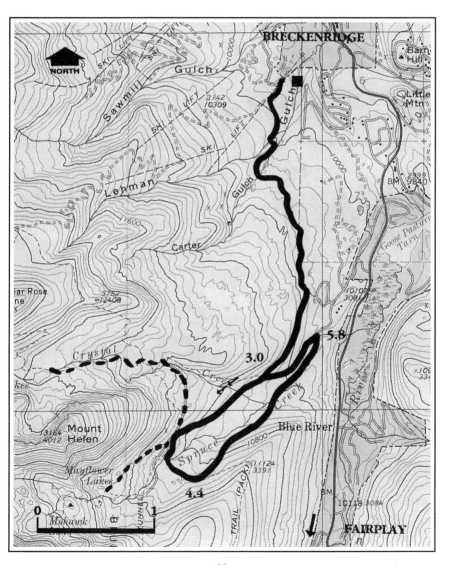

RIDE 6 WHEELER TRAIL SOUTH

DISTANCE: 18 miles
TIME: 4-5 hours
RATING: Advanced
ELEVATION: 9,600-12,480 ft.
GAIN: 2,880 ft.
TYPE: Loop;
trail/dirt rd./paved rd.
SEASON: July through September
MAPS: USGS 7.5 Breckenridge
TI Breckenridge South

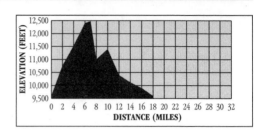

This section of Wheeler National Recreation Trail travels south along the slopes of Peak 10, Mt. Helen and Pacific Peak. Strong riders will enjoy the technically demanding terrain and county-wide views along this high alpine route.

ACCESS: Drive through Breckenridge on HWY 9. Turn right at the stoplight at the south end of town onto South Park Avenue and park in the large lot on the right, behind JohSha's.

DESCRIPTION: Follow Village Road (accessed across from the parking lot) toward Peak 9. Turn left into and pedal through the parking lot below Beaver Run Resort. Fork right onto the ski area access road that climbs Peak 9. It veers right, winding under the Mercury chairlift and passing two side roads on the right. Stay on the main route which switchbacks upward beneath the Quicksilver chairlift. After passing a fork on the left, the road winds up Peak 9. A switchback to the right and two spurs on the left signal the final stretch before the day lodge **(3.4 mi)**. Continue climbing, passing behind another chairlift and a spur on the right. Switchback above timberline, often over technical terrain. Intersect the Wheeler Trail, which is marked by a sign and cairns **(5.5 mi)**. (The road continues on to Peak 10.) Turn left onto the trail (see ride 7 to follow it north) and cross a soggy, willow-filled meadow that may require walking. Climb along an exposed slope to the high point. The trail winds along through tundra (stay on the designated route to prevent damage to fragile vegetation) and drops into the Crystal Lakes drainage. Descending along a steep slope, this narrow path is not for the fainthearted. Cross the Crystal Lakes jeep road **(7.5 mi)**. Climb briefly, then drop to Crystal Creek. Descend through the trees, often over steep rocky sections that require skilled maneuvering. Connect with a road, turn right and descend to the Spruce Creek jeep route **(8.2 mi)**. The signed trail continues on the other side of this road, dropping into a drainage. Ford three streams and intersect Spruce Creek Trail **(8.7 mi)**. (See option.) Stay on the Wheeler Trail which climbs through dense forest over a few steep pitches that may require walking. The gradient lessens as trail traverses a sparsely forested slope. A final descent into McCullough Gulch contains several extremely radical pitches. Connect with a dirt road **(11 mi)**. Turn left, then left again a short distance later and descend along a rough double track until joining HWY 9. Turn left and descend toward Breckenridge and to your vehicle.

OPTION: To create a shorter loop (14 miles total distance) use the directions for ride 5 from the point where the Wheeler and Spruce Creek Trails intersect.

COMMENTS: Get an early start; the exposed terrain provides little shelter from thunderstorms. Yield to the many hikers using this route.

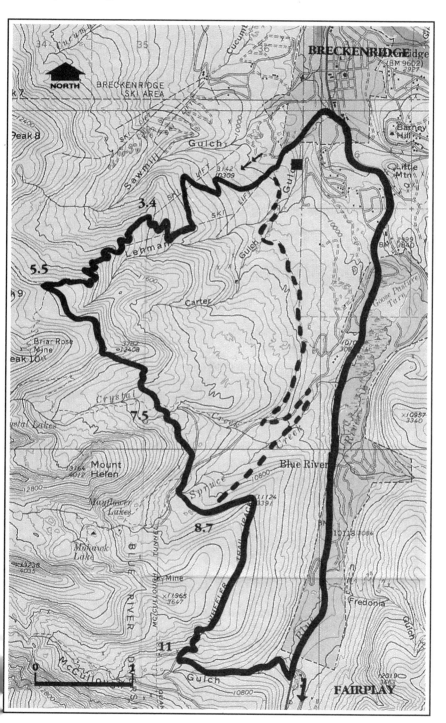

DISTANCE: 26 miles
TIME: 5 hours
RATING: Advanced
ELEVATION: 9,100-12,408 ft.
GAIN: 3,308 ft.
TYPE: Loop;
dirt rd./bike path/paved rd.
SEASON: July through September
MAPS: USGS 7.5 Breckenridge-Copper Mtn.-Vail Pass-Frisco
TI Breckenridge South-Vail/Frisco/Dillon

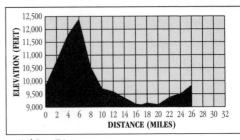

Covering a large portion of Summit County, this segment of the historic Wheeler National Recreation Trail contains a challenging ascent and descent over the Ten Mile Range and outstanding riding through high alpine meadows offering panoramic views of Summit County's mountains.

ACCESS: Drive through Breckenridge on HWY 9. Turn right at the stoplight on the south end of town onto South Park Avenue. Turn left onto Village Road and follow it to a parking lot on the left below Beaver Run Resort. Park near the ski slope and trailhead sign.

DESCRIPTION: Follow the ski area access road that leaves the parking lot and climbs Peak 9. It veers right, winding under the Mercury chairlift and passing two side roads on the right. Stay on the main route which switchbacks upward beneath the Quicksilver chairlift. After passing a fork on the left, the road winds up Peak 9. A switchback to the right and two spurs on the left signal the final stretch before the day lodge (**3.4 mi**). Continue climbing, passing behind another chairlift and a spur on the right. Switchback above timberline, often over technical terrain. Intersect the Wheeler Trail, which is marked by a sign and cairns (**5.5 mi**). (The road continues on to Peak 10). Turn right onto the trail (see ride 6 to follow it south) and contour across the tundra, being careful to stay on the designated route to avoid damage to the fragile high alpine vegetation. This narrow path climbs to a saddle between Peaks 8 and 9. The last .5 miles switchback steeply and require walking. Plan on spending some time on the pass (**6.2 mi**) to appreciate the views and effort you put into getting there. The trail drops steeply toward Copper Mountain. Radical dropoffs and stream crossings necessitate the need for caution on this challenging but fully rideable downhill. Pass Miner's Creek Trail spur and descend to Ten Mile Creek and a bridge (**9.5 mi**). (See ride 37.) Turn right and follow a faint dirt road to the paved bike path (**10.7 mi**). Descend along the bike path to Frisco and continue on it until reaching Breckenridge. Follow access directions back to your vehicle.

OPTION 1: To loop back to Breckenridge via dirt use the Peaks Trail. See ride 35 for directions. Although the distance is approximately the same you'll expend more energy.

OPTION 2: To avoid riding the paved bike path and reduce the total distance to 11 miles, leave a shuttle vehicle at Wheeler Flats trailhead near Copper Mountain.

COMMENTS: Much of the Wheeler Trail is above timberline. Get an early start and be prepared for weather changes. Mountain bikes are allowed only on ski area access roads; stay off the ski slopes.

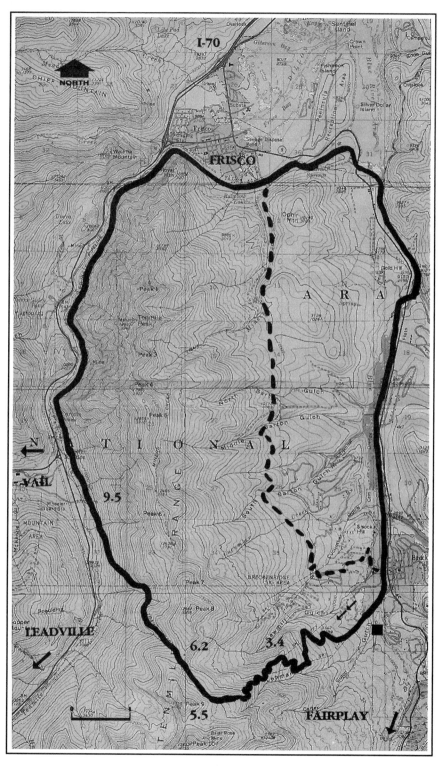

RIDE 8 BLUE RIVER TRAIL

DISTANCE: 9 miles
TIME: 2 hours
RATING: Easy-moderate*
ELEVATION: 9,600-10,040 ft.
GAIN: 440 ft.
TYPE: Loop; trail/paved rd.
SEASON: June through October
MAPS: USGS 7.5 Breckenridge
TI Breckenridge South

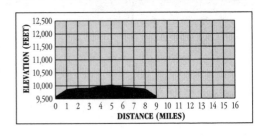

Beginning trail riders can polish their skills on this meandering single track as it climbs along the east side of the upper Blue River Valley.

ACCESS: Drive through Breckenridge on HWY 9. Turn right at the stoplight on the south end of town onto South Park Avenue and park in the large lot on the right, behind JohSha's.

DESCRIPTION: Pedal back out to Main Street. Turn right and follow the highway a short distance. Turn left onto Boreas Pass Road and climb to the first switchback. Fork right onto a gravel road near a cabin. (Beyond this point you're on private land until connecting with the highway several miles later; do not leave the described route.) After the gate, hang right onto a less-used route and cross the edge of a meadow. The road turns to trail, parallels a fence, then swings left and climbs a narrow draw. (Expect signs and improved riding conditions once trail maintenance begins in summer, 1993.) After some technical climbing you follow an old ditch, then drop into another drainage. Cross below a dried-up pond and connect with a main-looking route **(2.0 mi)**. Veer right and climb gradually along the left side of the draw, passing many spur trails. Eventually drop to a fence and the paved Indiana Creek Road **(2.7 mi)**. Turn right and descend briefly until connecting with the trail again, identified on the left side of the road by a sign. Turn left and descend, following the left fork which drops to the creek. Connect briefly with a paved road, then pick up the trail which continues up a slope to the left on the other side of the creek. Merge with a fork from the left, continuing straight. Ride along another old ditch. Steep dropoffs on the right necessitate the use of caution on this nearly level but narrow section of trail. Drop onto a main dirt road in Blue River subdivision **(4.2 mi)**. Turn left and follow Blue River Road as it winds through a neighborhood and out to the highway **(4.9 mi)**. Turn right and cruise down Highway 9 toward Breckenridge and to your vehicle.

COMMENTS: *The second segment of trail, narrow and sometimes technical, receives a moderate rating. Novices can avoid this part by descending along Indiana Creek Road to the highway. Do not abuse the privilege provided by these landowners; stay on the designated route. Encounters with other trail users are frequent on this popular path.

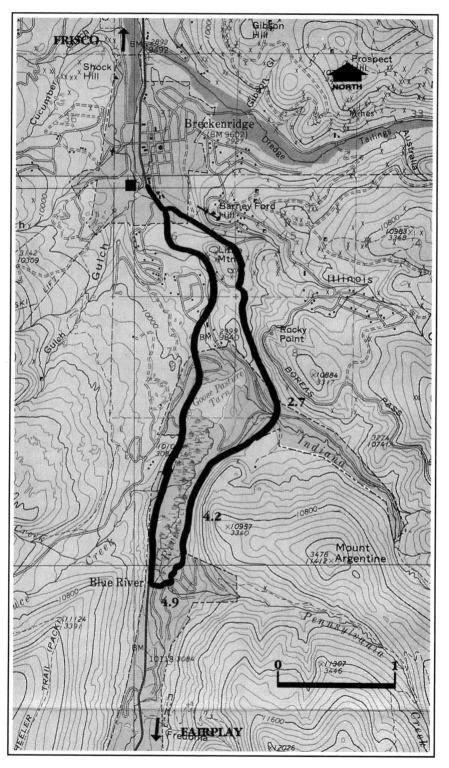

RIDE 9   PENNSYLVANIA–INDIANA CREEKS

DISTANCE: 13.5 miles

TIME: 3 hours

RATING: Moderate-
more difficult

ELEVATION: 9,600-11,200 ft.

GAIN: 1,600 ft.

TYPE: Loop;
dirt rd./trail

SEASON: Mid-June to mid-October

MAPS: USGS 7.5 Breckenridge-Boreas Pass
TI Breckenridge South

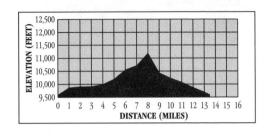

Interesting side trips, scenic meadows and spectacular mountain vistas highlight this popular ride.

ACCESS: Drive through Breckenridge on HWY 9. Turn right at the stoplight on the south end of town onto South Park Avenue and park in the large lot on the right, behind JohSha's.

DESCRIPTION: Pedal back out to Main Street. Turn right and follow the highway a short distance. Turn left onto Boreas Pass Road and climb to the first switchback. Fork right onto a gravel road near a cabin. (Beyond this point you're on private land until reaching the Pennsylvania Creek jeep road; do not leave the described route.) After the gate, hang right onto a less-used route and cross the edge of a meadow. The road turns to trail, parallels a fence, then swings left and climbs a narrow draw. (Expect signs and improved riding conditions on this first section once trail maintenance begins in summer, 1993.) After some technical climbing you follow an old ditch, then drop into another drainage. Cross below a dried-up pond and connect with a main-looking route **(2.0 mi).** Veer right and climb gradually along the left side of the draw, passing many spur trails. Eventually drop to a fence and the paved Indiana Creek Road **(2.7 mi).** Turn right and descend briefly until connecting with the trail again, identified on the left side of the road by a sign. Turn left and drop steeply to the creek. Connect briefly with a paved road, then pick up the trail which continues up a slope to the left on the other side of the creek. Merge with a fork from the left, continuing straight. Ride along a ditch and eventually drop into Blue River subdivision **(4.2 mi).** Veer left and ride past some houses. Turn left on both Royal Drive and Regal Circle. Take a final left onto Coronet. Climb along this road, switchback right, pass houses and ride into a large turnaround **(5.4 mi).** Ride up the jeep road starting from the turnaround. It switchbacks up into the forest, ascending steeply over loose rock for the first .5 miles. Soon the road levels and climbs into a valley rimmed by towering peaks. Red Peak, to the south, dominates the skyline. At a junction **(7.4 mi)** take the left fork. (See option 1 to continue straight.) Switchback up to another junction on the ridgetop **(7.9 mi).** (See option 2 or ride 11 to continue straight.) Turn left and descend through a series of switchbacks into Indiana Creek drainage. Pass a fork to the right, **(8.9 mi)** ride into the meadow and cross Indiana Creek. At the junction marked by a sign veer left (see ride 10 to explore this drainage) and continue descending. For awhile the road and the stream are one, look for trails on the right to bypass this. Descend to the property boundary and private firing range for Spruce Valley Ranch. Proceed on the access road which turns to pavement and passes a stable. Descend on the main road for another .7 miles beyond the stable. Look on the right for a fence and a familiar trail which you follow back to Breckenridge and your vehicle.

OPTION 1: To explore upper Pennsylvania Creek, take the fork that continues straight up the drainage from the lower junction. This rough road contains gradual climbs, steep hills and technical creek crossings. At a junction follow the right fork across the creek (the left fork is unrideable) and climb along this wildflower-lined draw to a high cirque. The route dead ends after roughly 1.5 miles of pedaling.

OPTION 2: Another 1-mile side trip starts from the ridgetop junction. Follow the spur that climbs south along the high ridge through the skeletal remains of a large burn. The road fades away after the second knoll. Views from this ridgeline are superb.

COMMENTS: Stay on the described route while riding through Spruce Valley Ranch and the Blue River Trail; you're on private property the entire time.

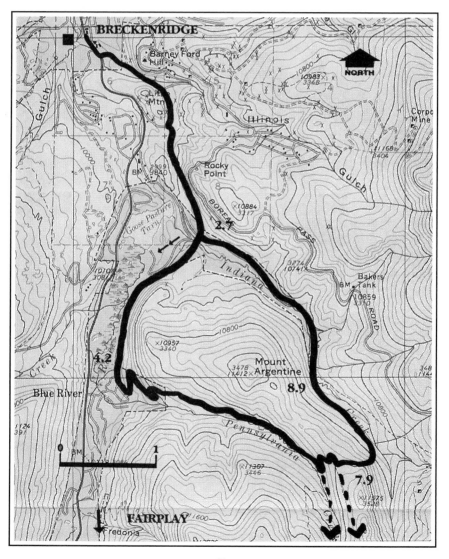

DISTANCE:	16 miles
TIME:	4 hours
RATING:	Moderate-more difficult
ELEVATION:	9,600-11,200 ft.
GAIN:	1,600 ft.
TYPE:	Loop; dirt rd./trail/paved rd.
SEASON:	Mid-June to mid-October
MAPS:	USGS 7.5 Breckenridge-Boreas Pass TI Breckenridge South

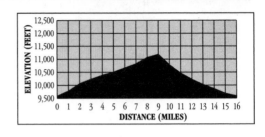

Dyersville, once a busy mining camp, sits quietly near the headwaters of Indiana Creek and is accessed by a network of dirt roads including the Boreas Pass railroad grade and a rugged jeep road.

ACCESS: Drive through Breckenridge on HWY 9. Turn right at the stoplight on the south end of town onto South Park Avenue and park in the large lot on the right, behind JohSha's.

DESCRIPTION: Pedal back out to Main Street. Turn right and follow the highway a short distance. Turn left onto Boreas Pass Road. Wind gradually up this road until pavement ends (**3.9 mi**). Continue on a well maintained dirt road which follows the old railroad grade toward Boreas Pass. Pass Baker's Tank (**7.0 mi**). (See ride 3.) Continue climbing, winding in and out of drainages along the flank of Bald Mountain. At about **8.9 miles** look for a fork to the right across the road from dilapidated cabin foundations. Follow this side road (see ride 2 to continue to Boreas Pass) as it drops into the Indiana Creek drainage over steep, rocky terrain. After descending for roughly .5 miles turn left onto the spur for Dyersville (**9.4 mi**). Pedal along a shady hillside for a short distance until dropping to Indiana Creek and the few remaining structures from Dyersville, which was founded by the famous "snowshoe preacher" Reverend John Dyer. Residents of Dyersville worked the nearby Warrior's Mark Mine (located a short distance further up the road). From the creek, backtrack to the main jeep road and continue descending. Reach an open valley and the spur for Pennsylvania Creek (**11.2 mi**). (See ride 9.) Stay right and descend to the property boundary and private firing range for Spruce Valley Ranch. Proceed on the access road which turns to pavement and passes a stable. Descend on the main road for another .7 miles beyond the stable. Look for a trail forking right near a log fence and driveway (**13 mi**). Descend on this single track, passing many side trails. Veer left near a dried-up pond, ride along an old ditch and eventually drop into an open area. Parallel a fenceline briefly, then connect with a gravel road. Turn left and intersect Boreas Pass Road. Follow it down to Breckenridge and your vehicle.

COMMENTS: Expect traffic on Boreas Pass Road. Stay on the described route while riding through Spruce Valley Ranch and along the trail; you're on private property the entire time.

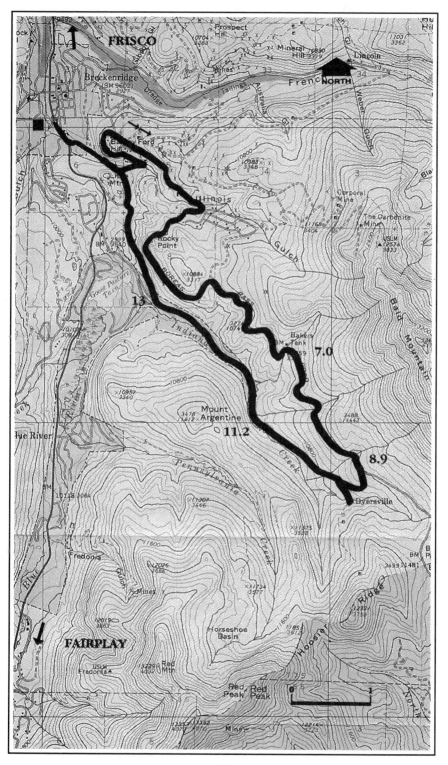

RIDE 11   HOOSIER RIDGE

DISTANCE: 26 miles
TIME: 5 hours
RATING: More difficult-advanced*
ELEVATION: 9,600-11,720 ft.
GAIN: 2,120 ft.
TYPE: Loop; dirt rd./trail
SEASON: Late June through September
MAPS: USGS 7.5 Breckenridge-Boreas Pass-Como
TI Breckenridge South

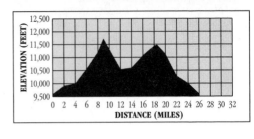

Combining the best of Breckenridge riding, this route crosses the Continental Divide twice, explores rarely used jeep roads and travels the popular Boreas Pass railroad grade.

ACCESS: Drive through Breckenridge on HWY 9. Turn right at the stoplight on the south end of town onto South Park Avenue and park in the large lot on the right, behind JohSha's.

DESCRIPTION: Pedal back out to Main Street. Turn right and follow the highway a short distance. Turn left onto Boreas Pass Road and climb to the first switchback. Fork right onto a gravel road near a cabin. (Beyond this point you're on private land until reaching Pennsylvania Creek jeep road; do not leave the described route.) After the gate, hang right onto a less-used route and cross the edge of a meadow. The road turns to trail, parallels a fence, then swings left and climbs a narrow draw. (Expect signs and improved riding conditions on this first section once trail maintenance begins in summer, 1993.) After some technical climbing you follow an old ditch, then drop into another drainage. Cross below a dried-up pond and connect with a main-looking route. Veer right and climb gradually along the left side of the draw, passing many spur trails. Eventually drop to a fence and the paved Indiana Creek Road **(2.7 mi)**. Turn right and descend briefly until connecting with the trail again, identified on the left side of the road by a sign. Turn left and drop steeply to the creek. Connect briefly with a paved road, then pick up the trail which continues up a slope to the left on the other side of the creek. Merge with a fork from the left, continuing straight. Ride along a ditch and eventually drop into Blue River subdivision **(4.2 mi)**. Veer left and ride past some houses. Turn left on both Royal Drive and Regal Circle. Take a final left onto Coronet. Climb along this road, switchback right, pass houses and ride into a large turnaround **(5.4 mi)**. Ride up the jeep road starting from the turnaround. It switchbacks up into the forest, ascending steeply over loose rock for the first .5 miles. Soon the road levels and climbs into a valley rimmed by towering peaks. Take the left fork at the junction **(7.4 mi)**. Switchback up to another junction on the ridgetop **(7.9 mi)**. The left fork descends into Indiana Creek. (See ride 9.) Continue straight, climbing onto a ridge covered by the skeletal remains of a large burn. Pass a couple of viewpoint spurs on the left. On the south end of the ridge, beyond the second knoll, the road fades away. Curve right on a faint track that continues south along the ridge toward treeline where it connects with a rugged jeep road. Turn left and climb strenuously through the trees to a junction **(9.2 mi)**. Turn left and descend to an exposed saddle and another junction on Hoosier Ridge. Fork right and descend toward South Park. Steep at first, the gradient soon levels, twisting in and out of trees, open meadows and over small creeks. Pass several spurs forking to campsites. Continue on the main road which drops to North Tarryall Creek and cruises along the left side of a drainage full of beaver ponds and willows. Reach Selkirk Campground and a major 3-way intersection **(13.1 mi)**. Veer left and switchback up to Boreas Pass Road. Turn left and climb gradually for almost 4 miles until reaching the pass. Then cruise downhill for roughly 1.5 miles and turn left onto the access road for Indiana Creek. Descend steeply over rocky terrain. Pass a fork to the left (see ride 10) and continue downward until reaching the Pennsylvania Creek spur **(21.4 mi)**. Stay right and descend to the property boundary and private firing range for Spruce Valley Ranch. Proceed on the access road which turns to pavement and passes a stable. Descend on the main road for another .7 miles beyond the stable. Look on the right for a fence and a familiar trail which you follow back to Breckenridge and your vehicle.

COMMENTS: *Distance and a short, technical climb necessitate the advanced rating. A section of this ride is above timberline; plan accordingly. Expect traffic on Boreas Pass Road. Stay on the described route while riding through Spruce Valley Ranch and the Blue River Trail; you're on private property the entire time.

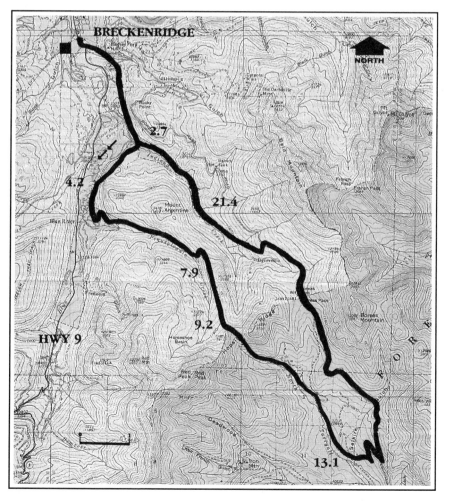

RIDE 12   FRENCH GULCH

DISTANCE:	13 miles
TIME:	2 hours
RATING:	Easy
ELEVATION:	9,600-10,880 ft.
GAIN:	1,280 ft.
TYPE:	Out&back; dirt rd./paved rd.
SEASON:	June through October
MAPS:	USGS 7.5 Breckenridge-Boreas Pass TI Breckenridge South

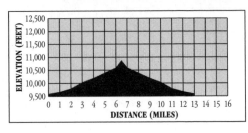

This well maintained dirt road travels through historic French Gulch, passing many fascinating mining remains. A beautiful mountain meadow is the final destination.

ACCESS: Follow HWY 9 south to Breckenridge. Park in a paved lot on the north end of Main Street across from Wellington Road (near Racer's Edge).

DESCRIPTION: Pedal across Main Street and onto Wellington Road which climbs out of town, curves left and heads toward French Gulch. At a 3-way junction **(1.5 mi)** turn right onto a wide dirt road. Initially well maintained, it climbs gradually along the left side of this heavily mined drainage passing many mines, tailings slopes and large piles of river rock deposited by dredges that scoured the streambed for valuable ore. Pass the impressive Wellington Mine clinging to the hillside on your left **(2.6 mi)**. One of the area's most productive, it yielded lead, zinc, gold and silver from 1887 to 1973. Large groves of aspen line the road and cover the hillside, lighting up the entire gulch in spectacular shades of gold during the fall. You'll pass many side roads; most lead to mines and private property. Ride among the few remaining buildings of the Lincoln townsite **(4.1 mi)** and past two major spurs. The left fork climbs Humbug Hill; to the right leads to Sally Barber Mine. (See ride 13.) Continue on the main road. Beyond a large tailings slope on the left that spills from the top of Humbug Hill, you ride through a gate **(4.8 mi)**. Continue climbing, passing a fork to the left for Little French Gulch. (See ride 14.) Beyond this point the road requires some ability to maneuver over rocks and through bogs and small streams. The ride continues at an easy pace over a gradual gradient, but beginners may have a few brief sections of walking. The road passes a few homes nestled in the trees and eventually winds into a meadow scattered with wildflowers. At the far end of the open area the ride changes to an advanced rating as it climbs steeply into the trees and up to French Pass. (See ride 15.) From the meadow, return as you came.

COMMENTS: Expect traffic on French Gulch Road; many people live up this valley. Respect the private property bordering much of this route.

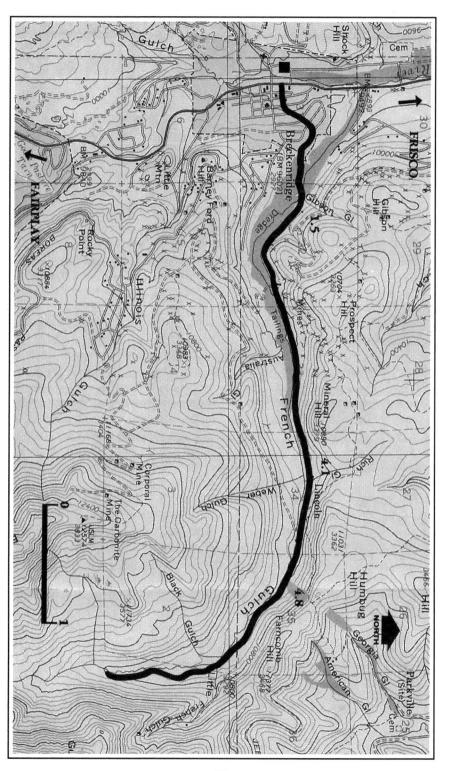

RIDE 13 SALLY BARBER MINE

DISTANCE:	9.5 miles
TIME:	2 hours
RATING:	Easy-moderate*
ELEVATION:	9,600-10,685 ft.
GAIN:	1,085 ft.
TYPE:	Loop; dirt rd./paved rd./trail
SEASON:	June through October
MAPS:	USGS 7.5 Breckenridge-Boreas Pass TI Breckenridge South

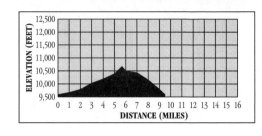

This scenic loop explores some of Summit County's historic regions including Sally Barber Mine, a well preserved structure perched on the ridge above French Gulch. The added bonus of beautiful stands of aspen make this a spectacular fall ride.

ACCESS: Follow HWY 9 south to Breckenridge. Park in a paved lot on the north end of Main Street across from Wellington Road (near Racer's Edge).

DESCRIPTION: Pedal across Main Street and onto Wellington Road which climbs out of town, curves left and heads toward French Gulch. At a 3-way intersection **(1.5 mi)** turn right onto a wide dirt road. Wind along the left side of French Gulch passing numerous mine sites and rock piles that remain from the dredging which took place in this drainage. Look for the enormous Wellington Mine on the left, **(2.6 mi)** surrounded by one of the many stands of aspen lining the road. Ride past the remaining buildings of the Lincoln townsite **(4.1 mi)**. Continue straight, passing a fork to Humbug Hill on the left. Turn right shortly after on road #2651 and drop to the river. (See ride 12 to continue up French Gulch.) The road heads back toward Breckenridge, climbing gradually for a little over a mile. Sally Barber Mine appears on the right at the high point of the ride **(5.7 mi)**. Much of the original mining equipment, used to recover valuable zinc from a 365-foot shaft, still exists. Continue on the main road, which descends steeply toward Breckenridge. After leveling, it contours through the trees past many side roads. Connect with paved road #520 **(7.3 mi)**. Turn right and descend a few feet. Just before a road forks left into the Juniata subdivision, look for the signed Juniata Trail taking off into the trees on the right of an old ditch. Follow this single track as it descends along a slope, eventually becomes double track and merges with a road coming in from the right. Continue downhill, cross another road and head toward the paved road. Curve left and parallel the paved road until reaching a 3-way intersection. Turn right, ride a short distance, then hang right again onto road #503. Continue downhill, veering left at roads #502 and #500. Descend until merging with Royal Tiger Road. Turn right, following this road until connecting with Wellington Road. Turn left and return to your vehicle.

COMMENTS: *A steady, 1-mile climb (and a short technical descent on single track) necessitates the moderate rating. Expect traffic on French Gulch Road; many people live up this valley. Stay on the designated route; most of the surrounding land is private.

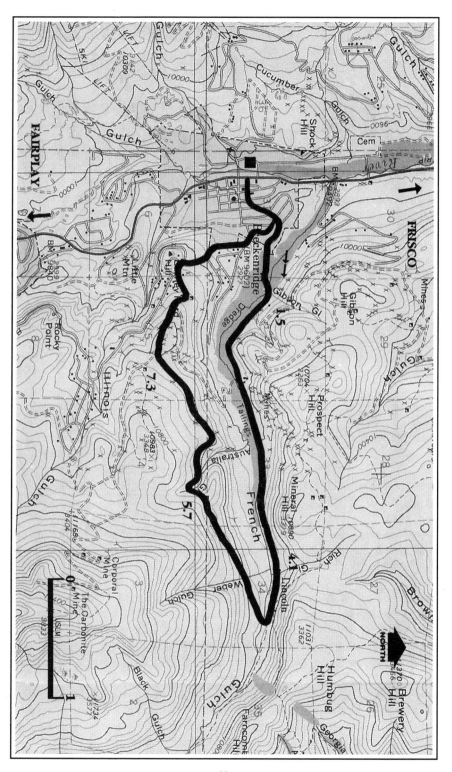

RIDE 14   FALL CLASSIC

DISTANCE:	15 miles
TIME:	3-4 hours
RATING:	More difficult
ELEVATION:	9,600-11,200 ft.
GAIN:	1,600 ft.
TYPE:	Loop; trail/dirt rd./paved rd.
SEASON:	Late June to early October
MAPS:	USGS 7.5 Boreas Pass-Breckenridge TI Breckenridge South

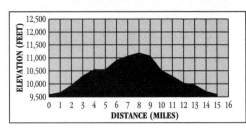

This route covers a variety of terrain and riding conditions, winding through many of Breckenridge's historic mining areas and following an old flume bed to the base of Mt. Guyot. Sections of this ride are used in the annual Fall Classic mountain bike race.

ACCESS: Follow HWY 9 south to Breckenridge. Park in a paved lot on the north end of Main Street across from Wellington Road (near Racer's Edge).

DESCRIPTION: Pedal across Main Street and onto Wellington Road which climbs out of town, curves left and heads toward French Gulch. At a 3-way junction **(1.5 mi)** turn right onto a wide dirt road. Ride a short distance and turn left onto a jeep road just beyond a private drive and across from a speed limit sign. (See ride 12 to continue up French Gulch.) Begin climbing as the road switchbacks left. Shortly after, take a sharp right and switchback up through aspen groves. Pass a house and fork right at the next junction. Climb around the south side of a hill, past mining remains and to a hilltop junction with roads connecting from all directions. Continue straight on the main road which climbs gradually through the trees. Pass a spur on the right and then two main roads that enter from the left **(3.0 mi)**. Continue straight and begin a .5-mile technical climb to the top of Prospect Hill. Descend along rolling terrain, continuing straight past all roads forking left and right. Ascend Mineral Hill, passing an old cabin on the right before reaching the top **(4.5 mi)**. Pass another cabin on the left. Descend on the main road as it switchbacks right, passes a couple of forks on the left and some mining remains. You eventually drop into the open meadows of Lincoln Park **(5.1 mi)**. Cross a creek and follow the main road which veers left and up into the trees. Climb steadily, eventually reaching a 4-way intersection near a collapsed cabin **(6.2 mi)**. Turn right and climb further to a 5-way intersection on Humbug Hill and close-up views of Guyot and Bald Mountains **(6.9 mi)**. Take the fork that continues straight and slightly left and climbs steeply up Farncomb Hill. Ascend a short distance, looking for mining pits on both sides of the road. Turn right onto a trail starting near a timbered mine pit. Actually an old flume bed which brought water to mines on Humbug Hill, this nearly level path contains some narrow and technical sections. Connect with a wider trail from above. Continue right on an old road, then link again with the flume and contour along the right side of the hill. At about **8.5 miles** you'll come out in Little French Gulch near the base of Mt. Guyot. Cross the creek and turn right onto a road. A jarring descent passes some cabins and drops along the creek until connecting with French Gulch Road **(9.5 mi)**. Turn right and ride down the main road for 4 miles to a familiar intersection. Turn left and follow Wellington Road back to your vehicle.

COMMENTS: Large stands of aspen make this a spectacular fall ride. Numerous side roads (most lead to private property) make route finding a challenge. Expect traffic on French Gulch Road. Expect changes from this description as future development and road improvements continue in private land holdings throughout this area.

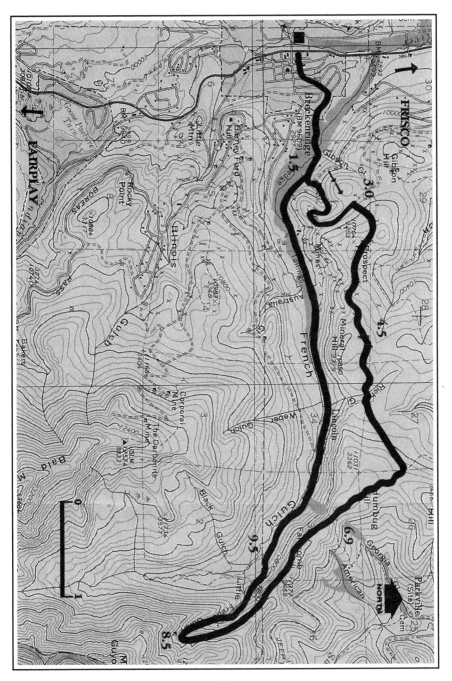

RIDE 15   AROUND MT. GUYOT

DISTANCE: 30 miles
TIME: 5-6 hours
RATING: More difficult*-
advanced
ELEVATION: 9,280-12,046 ft.
GAIN: 2,766 ft.
TYPE: Loop;
dirt rd./bike path/paved rd.
SEASON: July through September
MAPS: USGS 7.5 Breckenridge-Boreas Pass-Keystone-Frisco
TI Breckenridge South-Vail/Frisco/Dillon

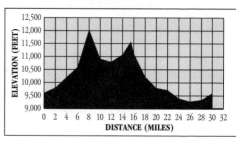

Two crossings of the Continental Divide and exploration along wildflower-covered slopes of remote French Pass highlight the circumnavigation of Mt. Guyot.

ACCESS: Follow HWY 9 south to Breckenridge. Park in a paved lot on the north end of Main Street across from Wellington Road (near Racer's Edge).

DESCRIPTION: Pedal across Main Street and onto Wellington Road which climbs out of town, curves left and heads toward French Gulch. At a 3-way intersection **(1.5 mi)** turn right onto a wide dirt road. Initially well maintained, it climbs gradually along the left side of this heavily mined drainage. Spurs branch frequently off the main route which remains obvious. Beyond a gate **(4.8 mi)** the terrain becomes slightly rougher. Pass several pine-shrouded homes. After crossing a meadow the road climbs steeply into the trees and through a gate. Technically demanding conditions dominate as you cross a creek and begin the strenuous climb toward French Pass. Full of rocks, this rarely-used route traverses wildflower-filled meadows below the rugged slopes of Baldy and Guyot. Reach the pass after struggling up several steep pitches that may require walking **(8.0 mi)**. A snowfield often obscures the faint double track descending from the pass. Occasionally reverting to trail this route drops along the left side of the drainage, staying well above the creek. Sometimes choked with willows, the trail veers left and continues downward. Faint at times, it requires sharp eyes to follow. Drop steeply into the drainage and cross two creek beds. Descend through a grassy area, keeping the creek to your right. Another steep drop brings you to the trees, French Creek and a gate **(9.5 mi)**. Cross the creek and climb to the right along an eroded section of road. Ignore the faint spur roads and curve left on the main route which climbs a bit more then descends, now high above the right side of the drainage. Pass a fork climbing right and continue descending on the main route. Connect with Georgia Pass Road **(11.5 mi)**. Turn left and climb moderately along this well traveled road for almost 4 miles to Georgia Pass. From the maze of roads radiating out from the pass (see option) follow the right fork of the two that descend to the north (marked by a sign for Breckenridge). Drop steeply, merging with a couple forks from the left. Continue downward along the South Fork of the Swan. Take the right fork at a junction just beyond a hillside meadow scattered with collapsed buildings. Continue descending. After fording the creek the road becomes more gradual as it descends past side roads and a house. You eventually reach a major 4-way intersection after crossing a bridge **(19 mi)**. Continue straight along the main road and descend until merging with Tiger Road **(20 mi)**. Turn left and descend. About .5 miles later the road curves left and becomes a well traveled route that passes mines, residences and a golf course before connecting with HWY 9 **(26.5 mi)**. Cross the highway and turn left onto the paved bike path. Follow this for about 3.5 miles to Breckenridge and your vehicle.

OPTION: See ride 21 for two variations on the descent from Georgia Pass.

COMMENTS: *Over half of this ride covers easy-moderate terrain but the ascent to French Pass, the descent from Georgia Pass and the ride length necessitate the advanced rating. Expect traffic in French Gulch and on Tiger Road and respect the private property in these drainages. Choose a guaranteed good weather day for this ride since you cross two passes and are above timberline for quite awhile.

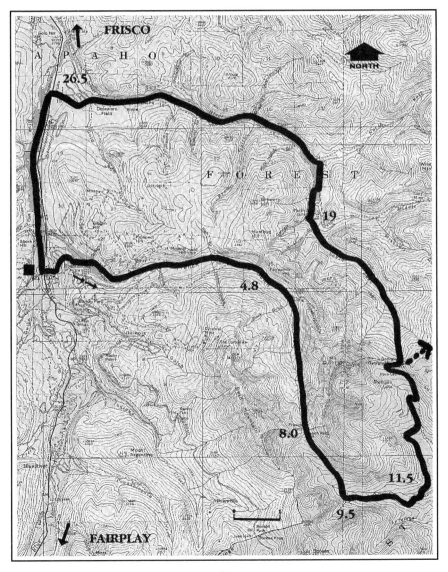

DISTANCE:	8 miles
TIME:	2 hours
RATING:	Easy*- moderate
ELEVATION:	9,280-9,920 ft.
GAIN:	640 ft.
TYPE:	Out&back/loop; dirt rd./bike path
SEASON:	Late May to late October
MAPS:	USGS 7.5 Frisco
	TI Vail/Frisco/Dillon-Breckenridge South

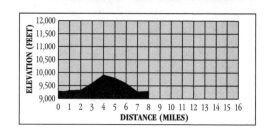

An easy cruise up Gold Run Gulch and through the Preston townsite offers pedalers a close-up glimpse of many well preserved mining operations.

ACCESS: From I-70, drive 7.2 miles south toward Breckenridge on HWY 9. Turn right onto road #400 (Fairview Blvd.) and park at the bicycle rest stop.

DESCRIPTION: Backtrack north for about **.5 miles** along the paved bike path. Cross the highway and turn right onto Tiger Road (by the Breckenridge Golf Course). Ride almost a mile and turn right onto Gold Run Road which winds along the left side of the course (watch for golf balls). Then climb above and away from it and into the trees. Ford a stream **(3.0 mi)** and pass the huge Jessie stamp mill, which was used to crush ore. Continue climbing, switchbacking right past a spur road on the left. More mining remains and several collapsed structures marking the Preston townsite come into view. Veer left on the main road and continue to a 4-way intersection. (See option and rides 17, 18.) Turn left and climb gradually past more crumbling buildings. Veer left on the main road, passing the first of several spurs on the right. As you descend the road becomes smoother and begins contouring along the hillside through a dense forest. At a 3-way junction **(4.1 mi)** take a sharp left and descend over rough road for a short distance before rejoining the main Gold Run Road. Turn right and backtrack down the dirt roads, onto the bike path and back to your vehicle.

OPTION: Intermediate riders can create a longer loop (total distance is 10 miles) and explore more of this area by continuing straight at the 4-way intersection. Climb moderately for another .8 miles to the crest of Gibson Hill. After descending roughly 1.6 miles along aspen-covered hillsides, switchback right and drop onto the well traveled French Gulch Road. Fork right and descend to a junction. Turn right again onto pavement and pedal through a neighborhood. At the next intersection turn left and descend to HWY 9. Cross the highway and veer right onto the bike path which loops back to your vehicle.

COMMENTS: *A short, rocky descent presents the only challenge for novice pedalers. Expect some 4WD traffic on Gold Run Road. Snow melts quickly in this area, creating decent early season riding conditions. Expect changes from this description as future development and road improvements continue in private land holdings throughout this area.

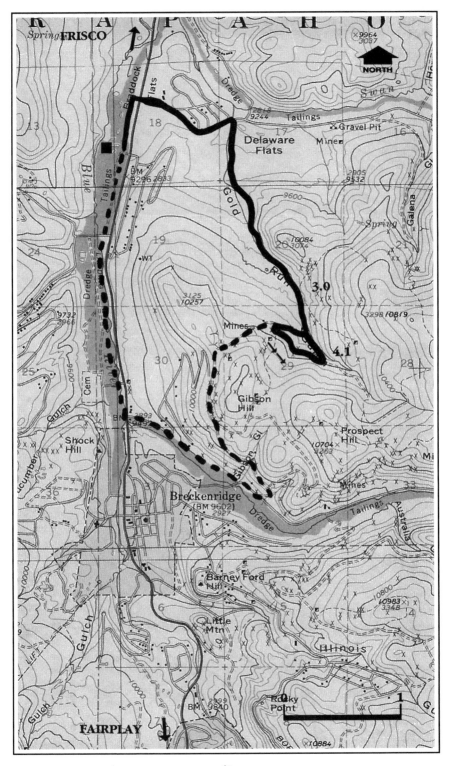

DISTANCE: 13 miles
TIME: 3 hours
RATING: Moderate*-
more difficult
ELEVATION: 9,280-10,280 ft.
GAIN: 1,000 ft.
TYPE: Out&back/loop;
dirt rd./bike path
SEASON: June through October
MAPS: USGS 7.5 Frisco-Breckenridge
TI Breckenridge South-Vail/Frisco/Dillon

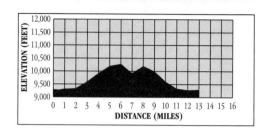

Golden Horseshoe ridge, bordered by two of the most heavily mined drainages in Summit County, is scattered with crumbling historic remains from the era when this region was swarming with energetic prospectors.

ACCESS: From I-70, drive 7.2 miles south toward Breckenridge on HWY 9. Turn right onto road #400 (Fairview Blvd.) and park at the bicycle rest stop.

DESCRIPTION: Backtrack north for about **.5 miles** along the paved bike path. Cross the highway and turn right onto Tiger Road (by the Breckenridge Golf Course). Ride almost a mile and turn right onto Gold Run Road which winds along the left side of the course (watch for golf balls). Then climb above and away from it and into the trees. Ford a stream **(3.0 mi)** and pass the huge Jessie stamp mill, which was used to crush ore. Continue climbing, switchbacking right past a spur road on the left. More mining remains and several collapsed structures marking the Preston townsite come into view. Veer left on the main road and continue straight at a 4-way intersection. Climb more steeply, passing a couple side roads before reaching the crest of Gibson Hill **(4.5 mi)**. Contour along an aspen-covered hillside and continue straight at a 4-way intersection marked by a private driveway on the left. As the road begins descending, look for a main-looking road that forks left **(5.1 mi)**. (Just past a less-used spur and usually marked by an orange arrow.) Turn here and climb a short steep hill. Curve left on the main road and wind through the trees. The next few miles pass many spurs; the described route follows the most traveled road and remains fairly obvious. At a 3-way intersection turn right. Pass more faint spurs and turn left at the next intersection. Descend briefly; then climb to an open area with expansive views of Breckenridge Ski Area and the Ten Mile Range. Continue on the main road which descends through some muddy areas, passes a road forking right and climbs to a side road on the right **(6.1 mi)**. Turn onto this spur which connects shortly with another well-used road. Turn right again and descend. Contour along a forested hillside and onto a knoll overlooking French Gulch. From the many roads converging at this hilltop junction, follow the main route which descends beyond the knoll. Begin a one-mile downhill cruise past mine sites, distinctive yellow-colored tailings piles and a house. Switchback down an aspen-covered hillside; then connect with another road **(7.0 mi)**. Turn right and begin looping back up Gibson Hill. Aspen groves blanket this entire slope, providing welcome shade for a 1.5-mile ascent which alternates between short, steep pitches and fairly level sections. Beyond the side road marked with the orange arrow you are retracing the familiar route of Gold Run Road which leads back to Tiger Road and eventually, your vehicle.

COMMENTS: *This entire ride is moderate with the exception of two non-technical, 1.5-mile climbs. Lower elevations and large aspen groves create ideal early summer and fall riding conditions. Numerous side roads (most lead to private property) make route finding a challenge. 4WD traffic is a possibility. Expect changes from this description as future development and road improvements continue in private land holdings throughout this area.

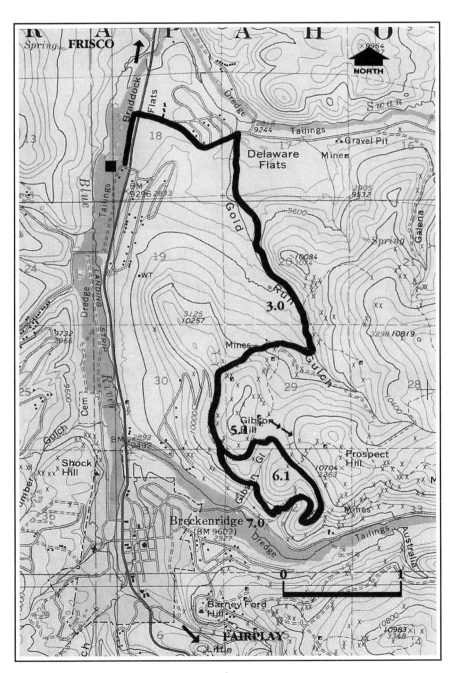

RIDE 18   GOLD RUN

DISTANCE: 12.5 miles

TIME: 3 hours

RATING: Moderate-more difficult

ELEVATION: 9,280-10,600 ft.

GAIN: 1,320 ft.

TYPE: Loop; dirt rd./bike path

SEASON: June to mid-October

MAPS: USGS 7.5 Breckenridge-Frisco
TI Vail/Frisco/Dillon-Breckenridge South

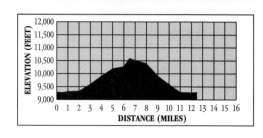

The Gold Run area is crisscrossed with roads and full of historic relics left over from the days when this region was a flurry of mining activity.

ACCESS: From I-70, drive 7.2 miles south toward Breckenridge on HWY 9. Turn right onto road #400 (Fairview Blvd.) and park at the bicycle rest stop.

DESCRIPTION: Backtrack north for about **.5 miles** along the paved bike path. Cross the highway and turn right onto Tiger Road (by the Breckenridge Golf Course). Ride almost a mile and turn right onto Gold Run Road, which winds along the left side of the course (watch for golf balls). Then climb above and away from it and into the trees. Ford a stream **(3.0 mi)** and pass the huge Jessie stamp mill, which was used to crush ore. Continue climbing, switchbacking right past a spur road on the left. More mining remains and several collapsed structures marking the Preston townsite come into view. Veer left on the main road and continue straight at a 4-way intersection. Climb more steeply, passing a couple side roads before reaching the crest of Gibson Hill **(4.5 mi)**. Contour along an aspen-covered hillside and continue straight at a 4-way intersection marked by a private driveway on the left. As the road begins descending, look for a main-looking road that forks left **(5.1)**. (Just past a less-used spur and usually marked by an orange arrow.) Turn here and climb a short steep hill. Curve left on the main road and wind through the trees. The next few miles pass many spurs; the described route follows the most traveled road and remains fairly obvious. At a 3-way junction, turn right. Pass more faint spurs and turn left at the next intersection. Descend briefly; then climb to an open area with expansive views of Breckenridge Ski Area and the Ten Mile Range. Continue on the main road which descends through some muddy areas, passes a road forking right and climbs past two more side roads on right (see ride 17) before curving left. A rough, half-mile climb brings you to the top of Prospect Hill **(6.5 mi)**. Descend for about .5 miles over rolling terrain and turn left onto a rock-filled road that drops steeply. (See ride 14 to continue straight.) After descending for another half-mile take a sharp right onto a less-used road and climb. Curve left and contour through the trees until reaching a junction **(7.8 mi)**. Turn left and descend steeply. Cross a small creek, pass remains of collapsed buildings and connect with another road. Turn right and resume descending. Stay right at the next junction and continue downhill past a spur on the right marked by No Trespassing signs. Take the right fork at the next junction and drop over rough road for a short distance until joining the main Gold Run Road. Turn right and backtrack down the dirt roads, onto the bike path and back to your vehicle.

COMMENTS: Snow melts quickly in this area, creating decent early season riding conditions. Numerous side roads (most lead to private property) make route finding a challenge. 4WD traffic is a possibility. Expect changes from this description as future development and road improvements continue in private land holdings throughout this area.

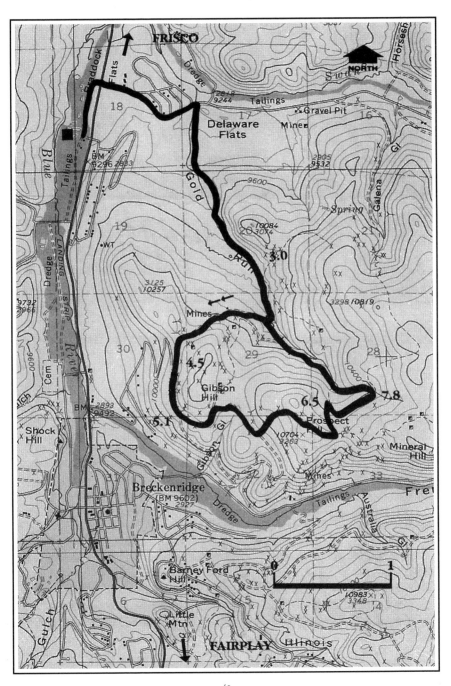

RIDE 19   SWAN RIVER LOOP

DISTANCE: 10 miles

TIME: 3 hours

RATING: Moderate-more difficult*

ELEVATION: 9,720-11,000 ft.

GAIN: 1,280 ft.

TYPE: Loop; dirt rd./trail

SEASON: Mid-June to mid-October

MAPS: USGS 7.5 Keystone-Boreas Pass
TI Loveland Pass-Breckenridge South

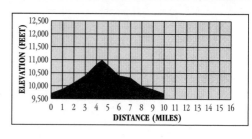

Using both the Colorado Trail and jeep roads, this route meanders through all three drainages of the Swan River.

ACCESS: From I-70, drive 6.7 miles south toward Breckenridge on HWY 9. Turn left onto Tiger Road (by the Breckenridge Golf Course). Drive 5.8 miles and park in a pullout on the right just before the North Fork and Middle/South Forks junction.

DESCRIPTION: Turn right onto the Middle/South Forks road. After roughly **.5 miles** turn right onto the South Fork Road. (See ride 20 to continue up the Middle Fork.) Cross over the river, veer left and pedal up the right side of the valley. Turn left at a 4-way intersection near mining remains **(1.5 mi)**. Cross the river again and begin climbing more steeply up the South Fork. Beyond a deserted house **(2.8 mi)** the road becomes extremely rocky but remains completely rideable as it passes less-used spurs on both the left and right (stay on road #222). After fording a small stream look for a rocky side road forking left **(3.5 mi)**. (Just before the main road crosses the river-see ride 21.) Turn here and climb. Loose rock and steep pitches make this the hardest part of the ride; you may need to walk. The road curves left and comes to a 3-way junction **(3.8 mi)**. Follow the left fork which turns to trail, crosses a creek near some collapsed buildings, veers right and climbs along the left side of the creek. Switchback sharply and steeply left and begin a short, strenuous climb. Descend briefly over a brain-jarring field of rocks onto a smooth section of trail that climbs steadily to a ridge **(4.6 mi)**. Negotiate some fallen logs and descend a very short distance until bisecting the Colorado Trail **(4.7 mi)**. Turn left onto this trail and descend further. Cross a flume (identified by its wooden remains) and continue switchbacking downward. The upper part of this newly-built path is wonderfully smooth. Further down a few rocky sections appear. At the bottom footbridges take you over a side creek and the Middle Fork River. Connect with the Middle Fork jeep road **(6.5 mi)**. Turn right, ride up the road a few feet and look for a continuation of the trail forking left into the trees. It may be difficult to spot. WARNING: Logging activity in this area during summer, 1992, damaged a segment of trail. Expect possible changes from this description once the route is rebuilt. A "closed" sign at the beginning of this section necessitates a detour by descending on the Middle Fork Road to your vehicle. This problem should be resolved by summer, 1994, at the latest. Anyway, this fun section of single track is relatively easy. It contains a few technical ups and downs but mainly contours along the lower slopes of Wise Mountain. Drop into a boggy, grassy area and cross a footbridge. The trail winds through the trees and is a bit tough to follow as it passes old campsites, eventually connecting with a dirt road **(8.8 mi)**. Turn left, merge with another road, descend through a gate and cruise down to your vehicle.

COMMENTS: *Although the elevation gain is moderate, there are several short but steep, technical climbs. You may see motorbikes on the initial section of single track and hikers/horsemen on the Colorado Trail.

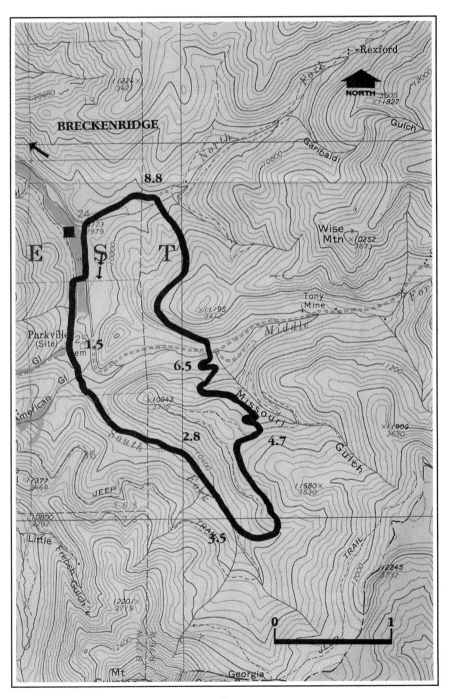

RIDE 20   THREE FORKS OF THE SWAN

DISTANCE: 9-10 miles

TIME: 3-4 hours

RATING: Easy-advanced

LOW ELEVATION: 9,800 ft.

TYPE: Out&back; dirt rd.

SEASON: Mid-June to early October

MAPS: USGS 7.5 Boreas Pass-Keystone
TI Breckenridge South-Loveland Pass

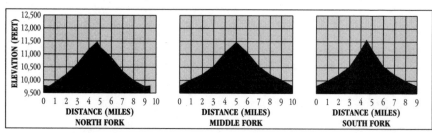

The North, Middle and South Forks of the Swan share a common trailhead and similar riding conditions. Each follows a jeep road up separate drainages of the Swan River into high country meadows containing remains of historic mining communities.

ACCESS: From I-70, drive 6.7 miles south toward Breckenridge on HWY 9. Turn left onto Tiger Road (by the Breckenridge Golf Course). Drive 5.8 miles to a junction. Turn right following a sign to the Middle/South Forks. Drive .5 miles and park off the road on the left at the Middle/South Fork junction.

NORTH FORK DESCRIPTION: This 9.5-mile, moderate to more difficult ride climbs 1,760 feet to an elevation of 11,480 feet. From your vehicle, backtrack down the main road **.5 miles** and turn right onto the North Fork Road. Ride along the left side of a meadow, through a gate and into the trees. Pass several side roads. The road splits just before crossing the North Fork River. You can take either route. They climb along both sides of the drainage, passing through recent logging operations before meeting again about 1 mile later. Continue up the left side of the river after the routes rejoin and past a main-looking road forking left. Continue straight on a narrow jeep road which climbs along a thickly forested hillside. After some short, steep climbs pass a group of cabins clustered in a small meadow **(2.8 mi)**. Continue climbing, now on more challenging terrain. As you near timberline the valley opens to reveal the cliff-like slopes of Glacier Mountain. Several collapsed structures near the road mark the site of Rexford, once a successful mining community. Alternating between rolling meadows and technical pitches, you climb toward a spectacular high alpine cirque. Turn around at a 3-way junction near a stream; both spurs dead end shortly beyond this point. Return as you came.

MIDDLE FORK DESCRIPTION: This 10-mile, easy to more difficult ride climbs 1,680 feet to an elevation of 11,480 feet. From your vehicle, take the left spur and contour along the left side of the valley on the Middle Fork Road. Ride through a gate. Climb gradually through the forest, swinging left on the main road. Pass several side roads and pedal up some short, steep pitches separated by level recovery areas. Beyond a junction in a hillside meadow **(3.4 mi)** (continue straight here) the road gets steeper and more technical. It switchbacks upward past the remaining buildings of Swandyke **(4.1 mi)**, a gold town which boomed during the 1890's. Climb into a beautiful timberline meadow surrounded by towering peaks. Pass a spur on the left and continue up the main road to a well preserved building perched on a steep slope. Beyond this point the road ascends over advanced terrain to connect with routes leading to Montezuma. Expect to walk a lot if you continue. From the historic building, it is recommended to return as you came.

SOUTH FORK DESCRIPTION: This 9-mile, easy to advanced ride climbs 1,785 feet to an elevation of 11,585 feet. From your vehicle, take the right fork and cross the river. Veer left, and climb gradually into the trees. At a major 4-way intersection near mining remains **(1.0 mi)**, turn left. Cross the South Fork River and climb more steeply along the left side of the drainage. Beyond a deserted house the road becomes extremely rocky but remains completely rideable as it passes less-used spurs on both the right and left (stay on road #222). Ford the river **(3.0 mi)** and take the right fork up the first of many steep, technical pitches. This marks the beginning of the advanced climbing that takes you to Georgia Pass. Beyond a gate the road passes a spur on the right and drops into a meadow containing several collapsed buildings. More steep climbs that may require walking bring you to Georgia Pass. (See ride 21 for additional riding suggestions from this point.) From the pass, return as you came.

COMMENTS: Expect 4WD traffic and respect any No Trespassing signs in the area. Spurs branching off these roads offer hours of additional exploring.

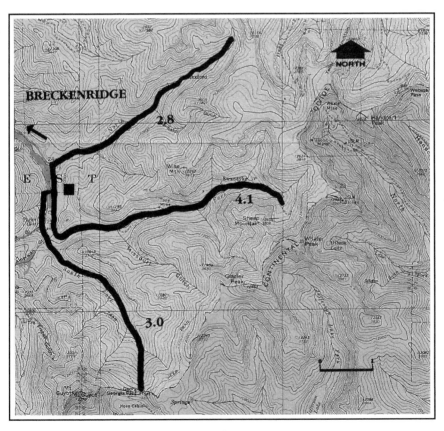

RIDE 21   GEORGIA PASS

DISTANCE: 10.5 miles
TIME: 3 hours
RATING: More difficult-
advanced
ELEVATION: 9,800-11,800 ft.
GAIN: 2,000 ft.
TYPE: Loop;
trail/dirt rd.
SEASON: Late June to early October
MAPS: USGS 7.5 Boreas Pass-Keystone
TI Breckenridge South-Loveland Pass

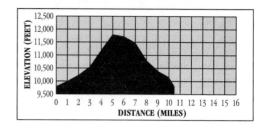

Expansive views from Georgia Pass enhance this superb loop which mixes rugged jeep road with newly-built trail for a variety of riding conditions.

ACCESS: From I-70, drive 6.7 miles south toward Breckenridge on Hwy 9. Turn left onto Tiger Road (by the Breckenridge Golf Course). Drive 5.8 miles to a junction. Turn right following a sign to the Middle/South Forks. Drive .5 miles and park off the road on the left at the Middle/South Fork junction.

DESCRIPTION: Follow the South Fork Road which forks right, crosses over the river, veers left and climbs gradually into the trees. At a major 4-way intersection near mining remains **(1.0 mi)**, turn left. Cross the South Fork River and begin climbing more steeply up the left side of the drainage. Beyond a deserted house **(2.4 mi)** the road becomes extremely rocky but remains completely ride-able as it passes less-used spurs on both the right and left (stay on road #222). Ford the river **(3.0 mi)** and take the right fork up the first of many steep, technical pitches. Beyond a gate the road passes a spur on the right and drops into a meadow containing several collapsed buildings. More steep climbs that may require walking bring you to Georgia Pass for a well-deserved rest **(4.5 mi)**. Roads head in all directions. (The main route continues down to HWY 285-see ride 15.) For this ride turn left onto road #268 which climbs a bit more through the trees before intersecting the Colorado Trail **(5.0 mi)**. Turn left onto the trail (see option to continue on the road) and traverse a tundra-covered slope marked by cairns. After dropping into the trees the trail meanders along a hillside, then down a ridge and into dense forest. The descent, broken up by many switchbacks, swoops along pine needle-covered ground and over unforgiving roots. Cross a motorbike trail **(7.9 mi)** (see ride 19) and shortly after, the wooden remains of a historic flume. As you drop deeper into the drainage the trail gets rougher and crosses several small creeks. Once over the Middle Fork River you connect with the Middle Fork jeep road **(9.6 mi)**. Turn left on this well traveled road and descend for another mile to your vehicle.

OPTION: For an incredibly scenic alternative which stays above timberline longer and adds 2.5 miles to the total distance, continue on the jeep road from the trail intersection. Pass some spurs forking right and contour along Glacier Ridge for several miles of spectacular riding in exposed, mountainous terrain. You eventually descend around a forested knoll and into a steep cirque. Below timberline the road becomes steeper and more rocky, creating challenging riding conditions. Negotiate one intensely steep drop by walking around on a trail that detours initially along the right and then on the left. Turn left at a junction near an old house, cross the Middle Fork River and connect with the well-traveled Middle Fork jeep road. Turn left and descend another 3.4 miles to your vehicle.

COMMENTS: Be prepared for exposure above timberline and the quick weather changes it can bring. Expect 4WD traffic on the South Fork Road and hikers/horsemen on the Colorado Trail.

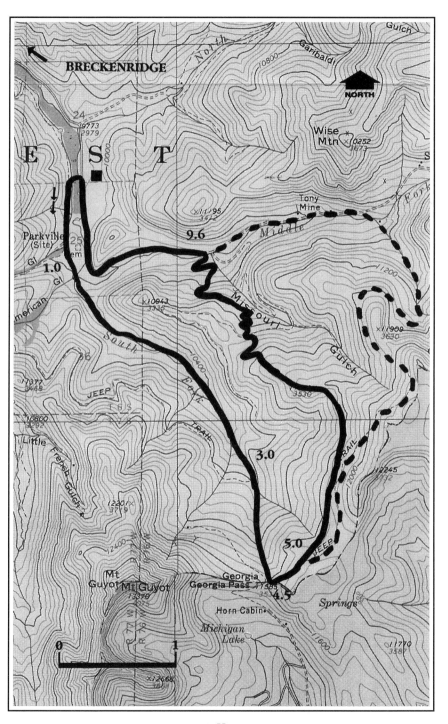

DISTANCE: 6 miles
TIME: 1-2 hours
RATING: Easy
ELEVATION: 9,040-9,360 ft.
GAIN: 320 ft.
TYPE: Loop;
dirt rd./bike path/paved rd.
SEASON: Mid-May through October
MAPS: USGS 7.5 Frisco-Dillon
TI Vail/Frisco/Dillon

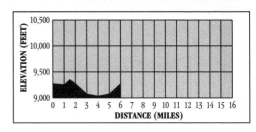

The rolling terrain of Tenderfoot Road is great for beginners. Following an aspen-covered hillside above Lake Dillon, the ride offers panoramic views of the Ten Mile and Gore Ranges.

ACCESS: Drive east on HWY 6 to Dillon. Turn left onto Lake Dillon Drive at the stoplight. Take an immediate right and follow a road that parallels the highway, turns to dirt and passes a water tank. Park in a pullout on the right by the Tenderfoot Trail sign.

DESCRIPTION: Ride up the dirt road and turn right immediately. Follow this fork past the water facility building on the right and up into the trees. Pass Tenderfoot Peak trailhead on the left and begin a series of short ascents and descents along a sagebrush-covered hillside. The route alternates between open meadows and large stands of aspen as it winds along the base of Tenderfoot Mountain. Breathtaking views of Lake Dillon and the Ten Mile Range highlight the next few miles of riding. At almost **2.5 miles** you encounter a 4-way intersection near the power lines. Turn right and follow the road as it descends past the Dillon Cemetery on the right and joins HWY 6. Turn right onto the highway. Ride a short distance and then access the paved bike path off the left side of the highway. Turn right and follow the bike path north as it curves around the lake and back toward Dillon. Merge with a paved road, veer left and descend past some condos. Climb a hill, heading toward Dillon. Turn right onto Lake Dillon Drive, cross HWY 6 at the stoplight, take a sharp right and return to your vehicle.

COMMENTS: Snow melts quickly in this area, creating good early season riding conditions. Large stands of aspen also make this an excellent fall choice.

Views of Lake Dillon and the Gore Range from Tenderfoot Road.

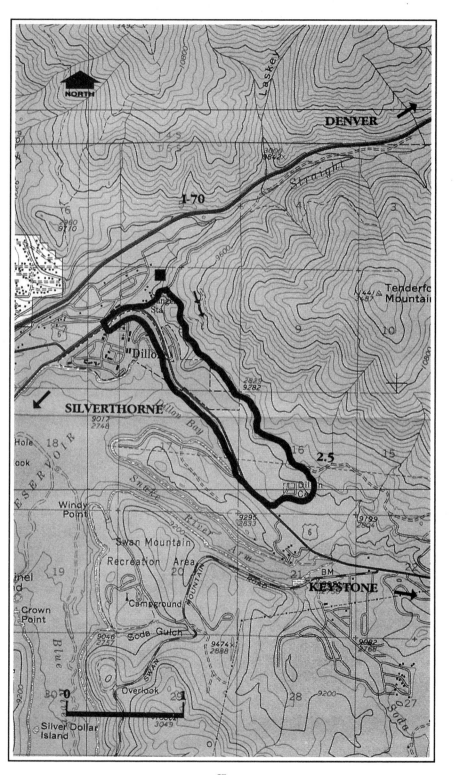

RIDE 23   SODA CREEK

DISTANCE: 11.5 miles
TIME: 2-3 hours
RATING: Moderate
ELEVATION: 9,000-9,500 ft.
GAIN: 500 ft.
TYPE: Out&back/loop;
trail/dirt rd./paved rd.
SEASON: Mid-June through October
MAPS: USGS 7.5 Frisco-Keystone
TI Loveland Pass-Vail/Frisco/Dillon

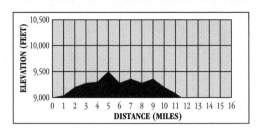

Following an old road which has reverted to trail in many places, this route explores rolling meadows and drainages east of Swan Mountain.

ACCESS: Drive 4.5 miles east on HWY 6 toward Keystone. Turn right at the stoplight onto Swan Mtn. Road. Drive .3 miles and park at the lakeside lot on the right.

DESCRIPTION: Backtrack on Swan Mtn. Road and turn right onto Cove Blvd. Go left onto Summit Drive and pedal through a neighborhood. After curving right, the road splits. Fork left and climb past an old cabin and a maintenance building to a metal fence. Veer right and parallel the fence. Where it ends turn left, ride a few feet, then fork sharply right onto a trail that winds up through the trees. (This new path, built for access between two proposed developments, will be easier to follow after receiving more use.) Climb a slope, veer left and cut through a clearing. Cross several confusing spurs, head back into the trees and descend along a wooded hill. Turn left onto a faint road, drop into a meadow (near fence posts) and merge with another road. Turn right and climb to the second log fence on the left. Turn left onto a trail (which is closed to motor vehicles), climb through the trees and descend to a boggy area. Climb back into the trees, through a hillside meadow and up a steep slope that may require walking. Descend to a road and turn right. Ride downhill along the edge of a sagebrush-filled meadow and back up into the forest. Descend again into the open and look for a trail forking left where the road curves right and climbs steeply. Follow this trail into the trees, over a hill of fallen timber and down to connect with the road again. Turn left and drop to a stream **(4.5 mi)**. Cross a log bridge and turn left at the 3-way intersection. (See ride 24 which explores the right fork.) At the next junction, turn right and climb a steep section of road that may require walking. Just before the top of the hill turn left onto a wide single track which drops into the trees **(5.2 mi)**. (See option 1 to continue on the road.) Descending through trees and along an open hillside for roughly a mile, this trail connects with a road near a pond and the old Keystone Homestead. (See option 2.) Turn left and climb along the edge of a drainage, passing the spur you turned onto earlier and shortly after reaching a familiar junction. Turn right and cross over the log bridge, returning as you came.

OPTION 1: To access Tiger Road, stay on the main route where the trail forks left from the hilltop. Descend through Horseshoe Gulch for about 1 mile to a gate and the Swan River. Fording the river and continuing on the other side brings you to Tiger Road, located a few miles north of Breckenridge.

OPTION 2: To explore another drainage and a remote hillside cabin, turn right near the pond and swing around the homestead. At the 3-way junction beyond the buildings and near a fence, turn right (the left fork leads to private property). Ride along the left side of a drainage on an abandoned road that eventually climbs more steeply, crosses a creek and switchbacks up a wooded hillside. It dead ends after 2 miles near a tiny creek where a trail forking left leads to a dilapidated cabin.

COMMENTS: This ride seems direction intensive but is fairly straightforward once in the area. Treat the Homestead as private property since it is used by Keystone Resort. Use this region ONLY during summer and only after June 20th to give the many muddy areas a chance to dry and to protect critical wildlife wintering habitat. Respect all private property at the beginning of this ride. A new section of Colorado Trail between the North Fork of the Swan and Horseshoe Gulch will provide numerous loop opportunities.

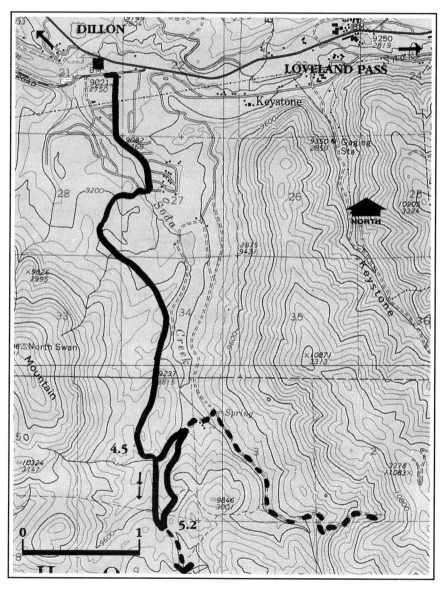

DISTANCE: 12.5 miles

TIME: 2-3 hours

RATING: Moderate*- more difficult

ELEVATION: 9,000-10,000 ft.

GAIN: 1,000 ft.

TYPE: Out&back/loop; trail/dirt rd./paved rd.

SEASON: Mid-June through October

MAPS: USGS 7.5 Frisco
TI Loveland Pass-Vail/Frisco/Dillon

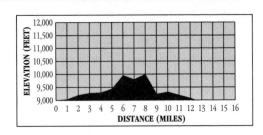

Ideal for after-work pedaling or half day rides, this route explores a secluded area full of sagebrush meadows and grassy drainages.

ACCESS: Drive 4.5 miles east on HWY 6 toward Keystone. Turn right at the stoplight onto Swan Mtn. Road. Drive .3 miles and park in the lakeside lot on the right.

DESCRIPTION: Backtrack on Swan Mtn. Road and turn right onto Cove Blvd. Go left onto Summit Drive and pedal through a neighborhood. After curving right, the road splits. Fork left and climb past an old cabin and a maintenance building to a metal fence. Veer right and parallel the fence. Where it ends turn left, ride a few feet, then fork sharply right onto a trail that winds up through the trees. (This new path, built for access between two proposed developments, will be easier to follow after receiving more use.) Climb a slope, veer left and cut through a clearing. Cross several confusing spurs, head back into the trees and descend along a wooded hill. Turn left onto a faint road, drop into a meadow (near fence posts) and merge with another road. Turn right and climb to the second log fence on the left. Turn left onto a trail (which is closed to motor vehicles), climb through the trees and descend to a boggy area. Climb back into the trees, through a hillside meadow and up a steep slope that may require walking. Descend to a road and turn right. Ride downhill along the edge of a sagebrush-filled meadow and back up into the forest. Descend again into the open and look for a trail forking left where the road curves right and climbs steeply. Follow this trail through trees, over a hill of fallen timber and down to connect with the road again. Turn left and drop to a stream **(4.5 mi)**. Cross a log bridge and turn right at a 3-way junction. (See ride 23 which explores the left fork.) Pass a spur on the right and ride up the left side of a draw. The road turns to single track and climbs above the drainage. Look for a difficult-to-spot trail forking sharply left about halfway through a steep climb in a hillside meadow **(5.5 mi)**. Turn onto this path to begin the loop section of the ride. Drop into the trees, around the edge of another meadow and up a steep slope that may require walking. Pass above a fence and descend on a "bobsled" type trail full of twists and turns until merging with another trail **(6.7 mi)**. Continue downhill, then veer right and climb along a forested hillside. Pass a spur trail dropping steeply left (it leads to private property) and climb further along the edge of a grassy draw. Pass a side trail on the right and continue to a saddle. Cross through a fence and drop back into the drainage where the loop began. Continue left on the main trail, returning as you came.

COMMENTS: *The majority of this ride is moderate with only a couple of short more difficult climbs and descents that are easily walked. This ride seems direction intensive but is fairly straightforward once in the area. Use this region ONLY during summer and only after June 20th to give the many muddy areas a chance to dry and to protect critical wildlife wintering habitat. Respect all private property at the beginning of this ride.

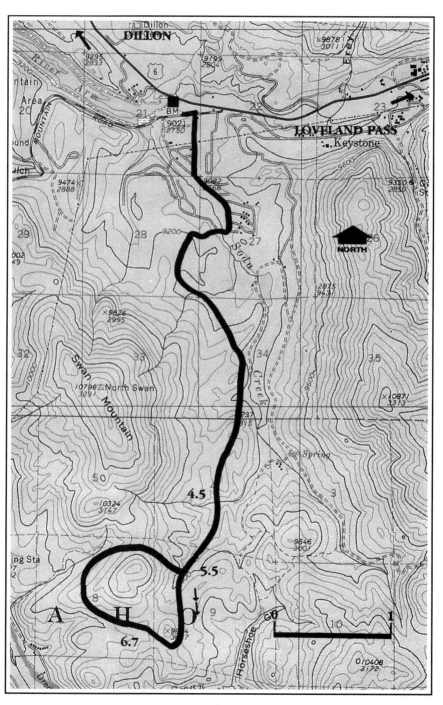

RIDE 25   KEYSTONE GULCH

DISTANCE: 14.5 miles
TIME: 3-4 hours
RATING: Easy*-
more difficult
ELEVATION: 9,240-11,920 ft.
GAIN: 2,680 ft.
TYPE: Out&back;
dirt rd.
SEASON: Late June through September
MAPS: USGS 7.5 Keystone
TI Loveland Pass

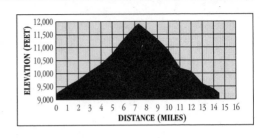

Keystone Gulch Road winds along the base of Keystone Mountain and up onto North Peak. Ideal for a variety of skill levels, the route covers several miles of easy pedaling before encountering more difficult terrain on the climb to Erickson Mine.

ACCESS: Drive east on HWY 6 to Keystone. Turn right at the stoplight onto Keystone Road. Take an immediate left, cross the Snake River and turn right onto Soda Ridge Road. Drive .4 miles and turn left onto Keystone Gulch dirt road. Park near the gate.

DESCRIPTION: Begin riding up Keystone Gulch. Pedaling such a well maintained road makes it easy to enjoy the surrounding forest and meandering creek. Wind around the base of Keystone Mountain and past North Peak base lifts **(3.3 mi)**. Continue on the main road, eventually curving left and climbing more steeply under the Wayback quad lift. Pass the Outback Express lift which services South Peak **(4.5 mi)**. Beyond this point the rating changes to more difficult. The main road veers left and climbs steeply up a drainage between North and South Peaks. Ascend steadily for 2 miles along the road switchbacking up the back side of North Peak. Just before reaching the top there's a fork to the right marked by a gate **(6.0 mi)**. Continuing straight takes you up a short distance further to the Outpost Restaurant, which is open for lunch during the summer. To reach Erickson Mine, fork right and climb another 1.3 miles over rocky terrain through a huge, high alpine bowl. Several well pre-served mining structures sit above timberline on a tundra-covered slope. Incredible views make this final climb worthwhile. The road basically dead ends beyond the mine. Return as you came.

OPTION: For a completely decadent cycling experience, ride Keystone's gondolas (they take bikes) up to North Peak and the Outpost Restaurant. Total riding distance is cut almost in half and other than the climb to the mine, it's all downhill.

COMMENTS: *The first 4.5 miles of this ride are easy. Expect some traffic on Keystone Gulch Road. Avoid ski area roads other than those designated for bike use. The spur to Erickson Mine is mainly above timberline; anticipate changing weather conditions.

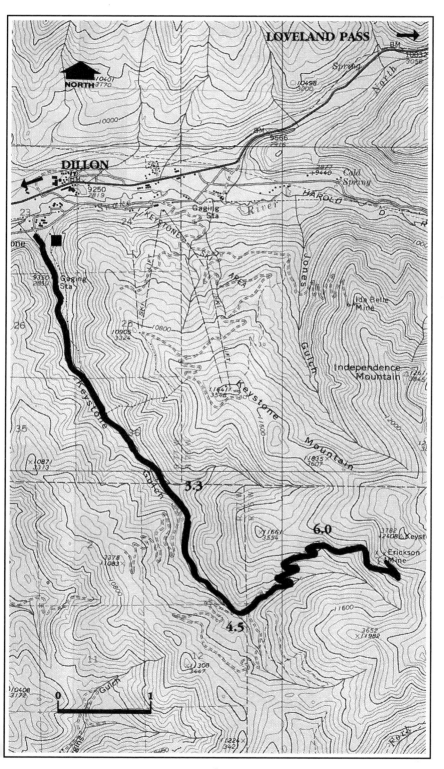

RIDE 26 WEST RIDGE

DISTANCE:	14 miles
TIME:	3 hours
RATING:	Moderate*- more difficult
ELEVATION:	9,240-11,100 ft.
GAIN:	1,860 ft.
TYPE:	Loop/out&back; dirt rd./trail
SEASON:	Late June to early October
MAPS:	USGS 7.5 Keystone TI Loveland Pass

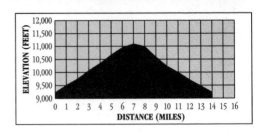

Combining a recently-built section of the Colorado Trail with abandoned logging roads in Keystone Gulch, this ride explores the eastern slopes of West Ridge.

ACCESS: Drive east on HWY 6 to Keystone. Turn right at the stoplight onto Keystone Road. Take an immediate left, cross the Snake River and turn right onto Soda Ridge Road. Drive .4 miles and turn left onto Keystone Gulch dirt road. Park near the gate.

DESCRIPTION: Climb along Keystone Gulch road for approximately **4.5 miles**. After it passes a chairlift and swings left to begin a steep climb up North Peak (see ride 25) turn right, crossing over a creek onto a spur near a maintenance building. Climb along a hillside for almost .5 miles, bisecting two ski runs. Take the right fork at a junction, drop into a willow-filled meadow and cross a stream. Climb along an abandoned logging road, pass a collapsed mine shaft on the right and switchback upward. Alternate between climbing and contouring, passing a couple of faint side roads. After a long level section, you reach a major 3-way junction **(6.0 mi)**. The right fork drops back into Keystone Gulch. (See option.) To continue the ride turn left and climb, continuing straight past two forks on the left. At the next junction stay left, then switchback left past a spur on the right. Climb past another fork on the right. The road weaves through an area almost completely overgrown with saplings, curves left through some fallen trees and dead ends **(6.7 mi)**. Continue straight on a faint path that merges a short distance later with the Colorado Trail. Turn sharply right and contour north along the trail. Cross gradually over West Ridge and wind along the other side until reaching a switchback **(8.0 mi)**. (See ride 27 for a continuation of the Colorado Trail.) Turn onto a faint trail that climbs steeply to the right. Pedal up a hill to the ridgetop and drop steeply down the other side, through a campsite and onto an old logging road. Turn right and descend through a series of switchbacks over sometimes rough terrain for almost 3 miles. (Ignore the many side roads.) Once in Keystone Gulch cross the creek, turn left and descend to your vehicle.

OPTION: A shorter loop which eliminates several miles, some climbing and the single track veers right from the 3-way junction on the logging road. Switchback downward along this spur, always forking right at any junctions. Drop into Keystone Gulch and cross the stream. Work your way around the left side of the chairlift and onto the main road. Turn left and descend to your vehicle.

COMMENTS:*Other than several short, technical climbs on the logging roads, the riding is moderate. Expect traffic in Keystone Gulch and both hikers and horsemen on the Colorado Trail.

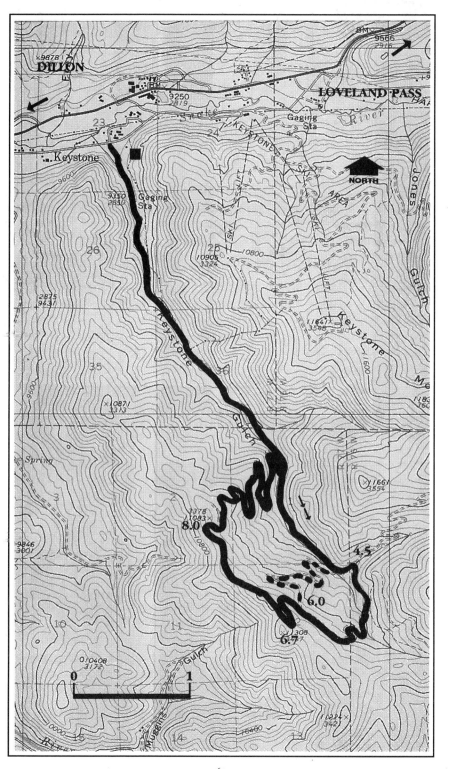

DISTANCE: 19.5 miles
TIME: 4-5 hours
RATING: Moderate-
more difficult*
ELEVATION: 9,000-11,100 ft.
GAIN: 2,100 ft.
TYPE: Loop;
trail/dirt rd./bike path
SEASON: Late June to early October
MAPS: USGS 7.5 Keystone-Frisco
TI Loveland Pass-Vail/Frisco/Dillon

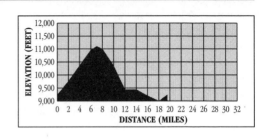

This variety-filled loop, which includes a segment of the Colorado Trail, crosses heavily forested West Ridge to link Keystone Gulch to Soda Creek.

ACCESS: Drive east on HWY 6 to Keystone. Turn right at the stoplight onto Keystone Road. Take an immediate left, cross the Snake River and turn right onto Soda Ridge Road. Drive .4 miles and turn left onto Keystone Gulch dirt road. Park near the gate.

DESCRIPTION: Climb along Keystone Gulch Road for approximately **4.5 miles**. After it passes a chairlift and swings left to begin a steep climb up North Peak (see ride 25) turn right, crossing over a creek onto a spur near a maintenance building. Climb along a hillside for almost .5 miles, bisecting two ski runs. Take the right fork at a junction, drop into a willow-filled meadow and cross a stream. Climb along an abandoned logging road, pass a collapsed mine shaft on the right and switchback upward. Alternate between climbing and contouring, passing a couple of faint side roads. After a long level section, you reach a major 3-way junction **(6.0 mi)**. Turn left and climb, continuing straight past two forks on the left. At the next junction stay left, then switchback left past a spur on the right. Climb past another fork on the right. The road weaves through an area almost completely overgrown with saplings, curves left through some fallen trees and dead ends **(6.7 mi)**. Continue straight on a faint path that merges a short distance later with the Colorado Trail. Turn sharply right and contour north along the trail. Cross gradually over West Ridge and wind along the other side until reaching the first of many switchbacks **(7.9 mi)**. Descend, at first through forest, then along a grassy hillside. Pass through a gate **(10 mi)**, descend back into trees and look for a tough-to-spot trail forking right in a flat area **(10.5 mi)**. (After completion in summer, 1993 the Colorado Trail will continue from here into Horseshoe Gulch and onto Tiger Road.) Turn right onto this narrow path and descend along an open slope. Curve right just before reaching the creek, climb briefly, then ford it and merge with an old road **(11 mi)**. Turn left and cruise down to a large valley and a major 3-way junction near a fence **(12.6 mi)**. Turn left (the right fork leads to private property) and ride past the old Keystone Ranch Homestead. Near the buildings go right onto a faint road and drop to a fence. Climb along the left side of another drainage, through a fence and past a spur on the left. (See ride 23.) Curve right and connect with a 3-way junction **(13.4 mi)**. Turn right and cross a small creek on a log bridge. Following a route that alternates between old road and trail, climb along another draw. Where the road climbs steeply left, fork right on a wide trail that goes around the knoll instead of over it. Descend and re-connect with the road. Pedal over rolling terrain through open areas and trees. As the road climbs again along the edge of a sagebrush-filled meadow, look for a well-used trail on the left.

(You've missed it if the road starts to descend.) Follow the trail over a hill, descend steeply to a meadow and eventually reach a boggy area. Climb a bit more, staying on the high trail, and drop to a log fence near a road. Go right and descend. Turn left onto a faint road (near fence posts) and climb briefly into the trees. Fork right onto a trail. (This new path, built for access between two proposed developments, will be easier to follow after receiving more use.) Climb a wooded slope and cut through a clearing. Cross several confusing spurs, head back into the trees, veer left and descend to a metal fence. Pedal along the east side of the fence to a dirt road and descend past a maintenance building and an old cabin. Turn right onto Summit Drive and follow it through a neighborhood. Go right onto Cove Blvd., then right again at both Swan Mtn. and Soda Ridge Roads. Curve right on Soda Ridge Road and merge with the bike path. Follow it over a hill toward Keystone. Merge again with Soda Ridge Road which takes you back to Keystone Gulch Road and your vehicle.

COMMENTS: *Length and several short, technical climbs necessitate the more difficult rating. Expect some traffic in Keystone Gulch and both hikers and horsemen on the Colorado Trail. Treat the Homestead as private property since it is used by Keystone Resort. Use the Soda Creek area ONLY during summer and only after June 20th to give the many muddy areas a chance to dry and to protect critical wildlife wintering habitat.

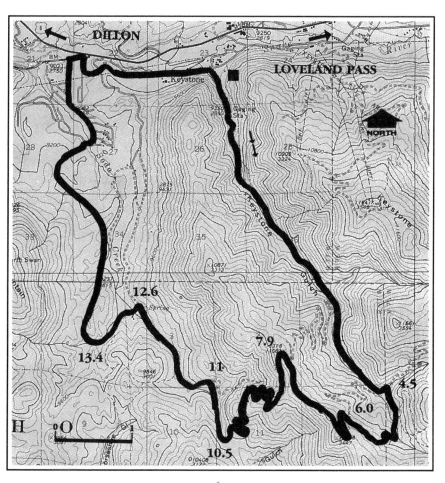

RIDE 28   FREY GULCH

DISTANCE: 8.5 miles
TIME: 2 hours
RATING: Moderate
ELEVATION: 9,200-10,120 ft.
GAIN: 920 ft.
TYPE: Loop;
dirt rd./trail/paved rd.
SEASON: June through October
MAPS: USGS 7.5 Keystone-Loveland Pass
TI Loveland Pass

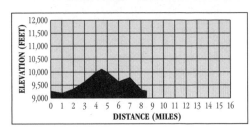

Easily accessed from Keystone, this loop travels along the lower slopes of Tenderfoot Mountain and up aspen-lined Frey Gulch.

ACCESS: Drive east on HWY 6 to Keystone. Pass through the stoplight and turn left onto an unnamed road just beyond and across from Keystone Lodge. Park in the large lot on the left.

DESCRIPTION: From the parking lot go right onto the highway and descend about a mile, passing through the stoplight. Turn right on Landfill Road which soon changes to dirt. Climb until reaching a well-traveled spur on the right just before the landfill gate. Turn onto this road, pedal uphill and connect with another road. Go right again, wind around the power station and up into mixed groves of aspen and pine. Descend along a logged hillside and across a cattle guard, passing several side roads. Shortly after crossing a creek you encounter a 3-way junction **(3.2 mi)**. Turn left into Frey Gulch. Pedal up this aspen-filled draw, again passing side roads. Veer right at a 4-way junction and continue up the gulch. The road gets rougher as it travels deeper into pine forest and across a creek. Turn right at a junction (the left fork ascends almost vertically to the top of Tenderfoot Mountain) and climb steeply for a short distance. Beyond a creek the road dead ends near remains of a cabin. Return along the same route until connecting with the main road at the bottom of the gulch **(6.2 mi)**. Turn left onto the main road and climb, curving left into a logged area. Drop to and cross over a tiny creek. Turn right immediately onto a faint trail **(6.9 mi)**. Turn and descend along the edge of a clear cut. Drop onto the lower (righthand) trail and into a forested drainage. Swing left, picking your way through the rocks. Descend along a hillside and switchback down to an old road. Follow this road through the trees, over a dirt barrier and onto paved Sts. John Road. (Stay on the described route once leaving the trail; you are crossing private land.) Turn left, following Sts. John Road to the highway. Turn right and descend to your vehicle.

COMMENTS: Expect horse traffic in this area. Frey Gulch is full of colorful aspen during fall.

An aspen paradise along Frey Gulch.

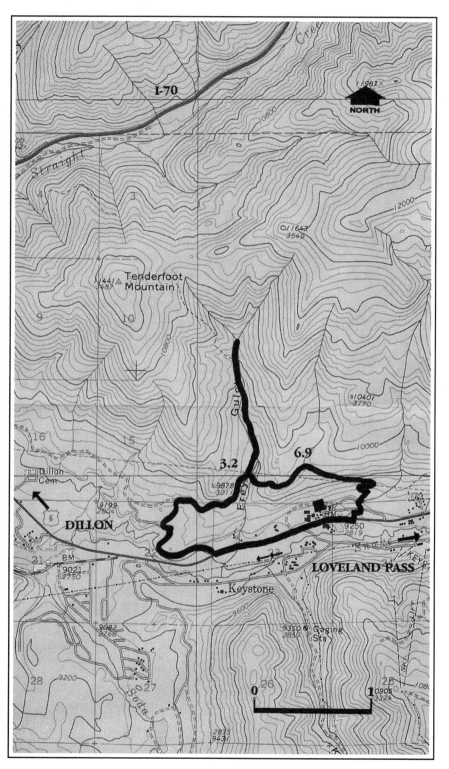

RIDE 29   PERU CREEK

DISTANCE: 14 miles
TIME: 3-4 hours
RATING: Moderate*- more difficult
ELEVATION: 10,000-12,120 ft.
GAIN: 2,120 ft.
TYPE: Out&back; dirt rd.
SEASON: Late June to early October
MAPS: USGS 7.5 Montezuma TI Loveland Pass

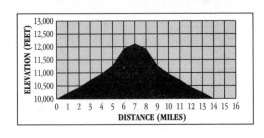

The ride through scenic Peru Creek valley passes remnants of many impressive mines, eventually ending in a high alpine cirque containing more historic relics.

ACCESS: Drive east on HWY 6 passing through Keystone. Turn right onto Montezuma Road. Take the first left toward Montezuma and drive 4.5 miles. Immediately after the road swings left and crosses the Snake River, turn left and park in the Peru Creek trailhead parking lot.

DESCRIPTION: Begin riding up Peru Creek Road. Cross Peru Creek and climb gradually up the left side of the valley. Pass a private residence and soon after, the Lenawee trailhead **(1.6 mi)**. Drop into a meadow and pass a sign for Warden Gulch marking a fork to the right. Shortly after, on the left, the spur for Chihuahua Gulch appears **(2.2 mi)**. (See option 1.) As the valley widens, Lenawee Mountain to the left and Collier Mountain on the right dominate the skyline. Ride past the grave of two young girls, Helen and Mary Clancy, on the left just before crossing under the power lines **(2.4 mi)**. This grave marks the area of the Chihuahua town cemetery. The town was destroyed by forest fire in 1889. A steeper creekside climb brings you to timberline and into a large hillside meadow. Argentine Peak and the Continental Divide fill the eastern horizon. The remaining buildings around Pennsylvania Mine appear on the right. (See option 2.) This mine was an extensive and productive operation, peaking in silver production during 1893. Continue on the main road and pass through a gate. Curve left near Shoe Basin Mine **(4.7 mi)**. Beyond this point the road becomes rougher and steeper, changing to a more difficult rating. Ascend through Horseshoe Basin, passing several spurs including a fork to the right for Argentine Pass Trail. The main route remains obvious as it climbs steeply over rock-strewn road, switchbacks left and comes to a junction near the head of the basin. Take the left fork, pedal another .8 miles and be rewarded for all of your effort with a pristine alpine lake nestled at the base of a talus slope. The road dead ends beyond the lake at a miner's shack. Return as you came.

OPTION 1: Chihuahua Gulch offers an advanced 3-mile side trip. A steep, rough jeep road/hiking trail brings riders deep into a remote valley bordered by the fourteeners, Grays and Torreys. Expect to walk sections of this trail beyond the point where it's closed to vehicles. Chihuahua Lake is reached by scrambling up a talus slope.

OPTION 2: The road forking right near Pennsylvania Mine climbs for about 1 mile over more difficult terrain into Cinnamon Gulch. After switchbacking above timberline, the route dead ends near a mine. View the many historic structures from the safety of the road.

COMMENTS: *The first 4.7 miles of Peru Creek Road are moderate pedaling. The final section is above timberline; be prepared for weather changes. This valley contains a lot of private land; respect all "No Trespassing" signs. Expect 4WD traffic, mainly on weekends.

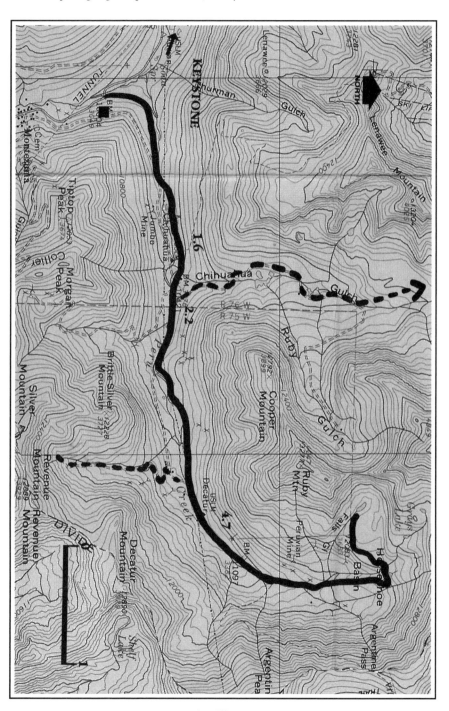

RIDE 30   HUNKIDORI MINE

DISTANCE: 7 miles
TIME: 2-3 hours
RATING: Moderate-
more difficult*
ELEVATION: 10,300-11,000 ft.
GAIN: 700 ft.
TYPE: Out&back;
dirt rd.
SEASON: Late June to early October
MAPS: USGS 7.5 Montezuma-Keystone
TI Loveland Pass

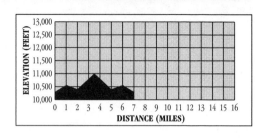

Hunkidori Road, one of the lesser-used routes around Montezuma, climbs through dense pine forests along the side of Bear Mountain. It eventually dead ends at Hunkidori Mine, located in a mountainside meadow.

ACCESS: Drive east on HWY 6, passing through Keystone. Turn right onto Montezuma Road. Take the first left and drive 5.5 miles into Montezuma (observe their speed limit). Park in a large pullout where road #275 forks right for Sts. John. (If this area is full or closed off, drive .5 miles beyond town and park at Deer Creek trailhead.)

DESCRIPTION: Ride up road #275, following the sign to Sts. John. Climb gradually up the mountainside, using several switchbacks to gain elevation. After about **.6 miles** turn right at a fork that drops to and fords Sts. John Creek. (See the option for a continuation of road #275.) Follow the route that continues on the other side, crossing a faint road and descending into the trees. Begin a fun section of technical riding over obstacle-filled, rolling terrain. Some extremely wet sections are made rideable by "corduroy road", a technique used by miners who laid wood across the route to make it passable. The road eventually veers left and begins climbing over "staircase" terrain which combines short, steep pitches with level recovery areas. A steeper, more technical section marks the final ascent before reaching the mine. Switchback left near a cabin tucked in the trees on the right **(3.0 mi)**. (Respect any "No Trespassing" signs in this area.) Hunkidori Mine, discovered in 1880, contained a rich vein of silver. Its remains are nestled in a small meadow at the base of some cliffs. The road dead ends just beyond the mine. Return as you came.

OPTION: You can continue on road #275 from the junction where Hunkidori Road forks right. Another .8 miles of moderate climbing brings you to the mining community of Sts. John. (All buildings are private; please view them from a distance.) Beyond town, the route becomes strenuous and technical. (See ride 32.)

COMMENTS: *Moderate due to its short distance, this ride has several short but steep and rocky pitches in the final mile of climbing. Expect horsemen and respect the privacy of those living in and around Montezuma.

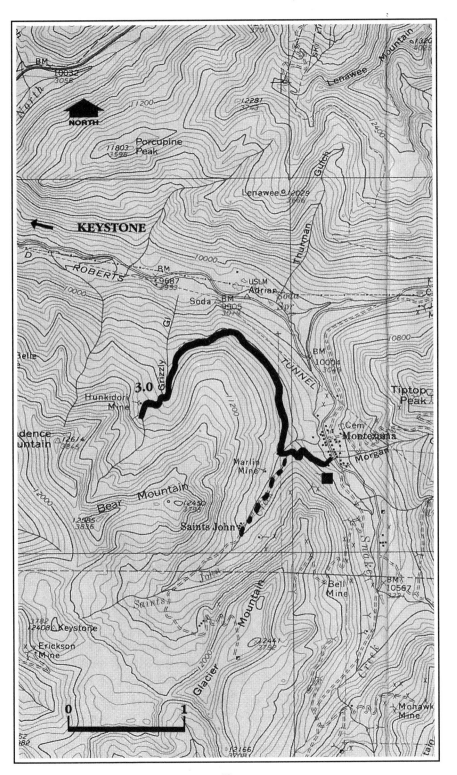

RIDE 31   WEBSTER PASS

DISTANCE: 10 miles
TIME: 3 hours
RATING: Moderate-
more difficult*
ELEVATION: 10,300-12,096 ft.
GAIN: 1,796 ft.
TYPE: Out&back;
dirt rd.
SEASON: Late June to early October
MAPS: USGS 7.5 Montezuma
TI Loveland Pass

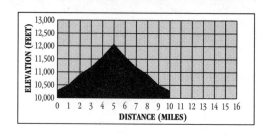

A moderate 5-mile climb takes you above timberline to historic Webster Pass, which crosses the Continental Divide amidst some of Summit County's highest peaks.

ACCESS: Drive east on HWY 6, passing through Keystone. Turn right onto Montezuma Road. Take the first left and drive 5.5 miles into Montezuma (observe their speed limit). Park in a large pullout where road #275 forks right for Sts. John. (If this area is full or closed off, drive .5 miles beyond town and park at Deer Creek trailhead.)

DESCRIPTION: Ride up the well maintained Montezuma Road (the main road through town). Turn left onto a rocky jeep road at the sign for Deer Creek/Webster Pass **(1.0 mi)**. (You've gone too far if you come to a large parking area.) Begin climbing, picking your way through loose rock and past several spurs leading to private property. Pass through a gate **(1.7 mi)** and climb into a beautiful high alpine meadow surrounded by towering peaks. Teller Mountain on the right and Santa Fe Peak on the left dominate the skyline. Cross the Snake River and proceed up the right side of the valley over several technical sections of road. A couple of aging buildings on the valley floor and yellowish tailings slopes, perched high on Santa Fe's slopes, mark the sites of many successful mining operations such as the Lucky Baldwin, Silver Wave and the Blanche. Reach a junction at roughly **3.6 miles**. The right fork climbs up Radical Hill. (See ride 32.) To continue toward Webster Pass turn left and begin a long, moderate climb up the mountainside, reaching the pass at **5.0 miles**. Perched on the Continental Divide, Webster Pass was originally a wagon route which provided an important connection from Montezuma to Denver and South Park. The road continues, dropping steeply to the southeast and eventually connecting with HWY 285. From the pass, return as you came.

COMMENTS: *Technical sections and sustained climbing necessitate the more difficult rating. The majority of this ride is above timberline; get an early start and be prepared for changing weather conditions. You may encounter heavy 4WD traffic on weekends. Respect all private property along the first couple miles of this ride.

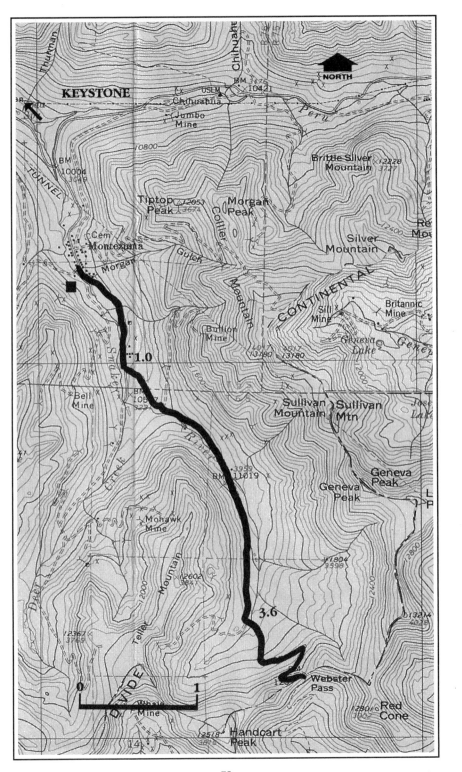

DISTANCE: 13.5 miles
TIME: 5 hours
RATING: Advanced
ELEVATION: 10,300-12,615 ft.
GAIN: 2,315 ft.
TYPE: Loop;
dirt rd.
SEASON: July through September
MAPS: USGS 7.5 Montezuma-Keystone
TI Loveland Pass

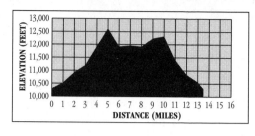

Riders tackling the steep terrain of some of Summit County's highest mountains are rewarded with peak-filled vistas, ridgetop riding along tundra-covered slopes and picturesque mining relics.

ACCESS: Drive east on HWY 6, passing through Keystone. Turn right onto Montezuma Road. Take the first left and drive 5.5 miles into Montezuma (observe their speed limit). Park in a large pullout where road #275 forks right for Sts. John. (If this area is full or closed off, drive .5 miles beyond town and park at Deer Creek trailhead.)

DESCRIPTION: Ride up the well maintained Montezuma Road (the main road through town). Turn left onto a rocky jeep road at the sign for Deer Creek/Webster Pass **(1.0 mi)**. Begin climbing, picking your way through loose rock and past several private side roads. Pass through a gate **(1.7 mi)** and climb into a willow-filled meadow just below timberline. Ford the Snake River and pedal along the right side of the valley. Reach a junction at roughly **3.6 miles**. The left fork climbs to Webster Pass. (See ride 31.) Continue straight toward Deer Creek and begin ascending Radical Hill which gets progressively steeper and more rocky. Beyond Cashier Mine the road switchbacks upward so intensely that walking is a necessity. From a lofty 12,615-foot perch on Teller Mountain's summit **(5.0 mi)** you look down on many of the peaks filling the skyline. Descend through high alpine tundra toward Deer Creek drainage. At the first junction, turn left and drop briefly until merging with another road that traverses the upper edge of the valley. A right turn here takes you down Deer Creek and back to Montezuma, an easy out if the weather turns bad or you're short on time. (See option 1.) To continue on the described route turn left and climb above the drainage to a signed 3-way junction **(6.5 mi)**. Turn right and follow the ridgetop road toward Sts. John. (The left fork drops into the Middle Fork of the Swan.) The next few miles are characterized by short, steep climbs and technical descents along exposed ridges. Pass a spur on the left that descends into the North Fork of the Swan **(7.2 mi)**. Veer right toward Sts. John. Approaching Glacier Mountain you pass a fork on the right, then ride/walk several steep pitches. After a final steep ascent, veer right and pass General Teller Mine **(9.7 mi)**, perched on the edge of Glacier Mountain. Climb over a ridge on the main road and drop into Sts. John drainage. A tricky, rock-filled descent brings you to treeline and past remains of Wild Irishman Mine. Continue winding downward into the valley on the main road. Ride through Sts. John **(12 mi)**, supposedly the site of Colorado's first silver strike. The last couple of miles you pass several spur roads but the main route remains easy to follow as it descends along the creek and switchbacks down to Montezuma, ending near your vehicle.

OPTIONS: This ride can be broken into two, shorter loops that originate and end at the same trailhead as the longer ride.

OPTION 1: Snake River-Deer Creek Loop: this 10.5-mile, advanced ride follows the jeep road up Radical Hill and over Teller Mountain, then descends along Deer Creek.

OPTION 2: Deer Creek-Sts. John Loop: this 12-mile, advanced ride continues on Montezuma Road past the turnoff for Webster Pass. It climbs along Deer Creek jeep road to a signed 3-way junction high above the drainage at roughly 4.5 miles. A right turn at this junction then uses the same description as the latter part of the Montezuma Loop, traveling along the ridgetops and into Sts. John drainage.

COMMENTS: Plan on walking several extremely steep pitches. Get an early start and anticipate sudden weather changes. Protect fragile mountaintop vegetation by staying on defined roads. Expect 4WD traffic, especially on weekends. Property owners in the area ask that you remain on designated routes and respect "No Trespassing" signs. These loops can be ridden in either direction; you'll encounter steep pitches any way you go. Deer Creek is the easiest of the three drainages to ascend.

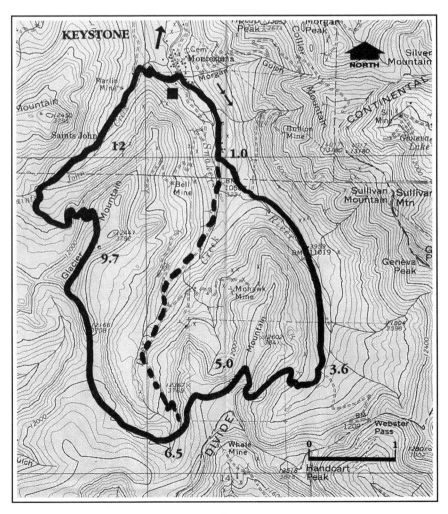

DISTANCE:	5 miles
TIME:	1 hour
RATING:	Easy
ELEVATION:	9,040-9,240 ft.
GAIN:	200 ft.
TYPE:	Out&back; dirt rd.
SEASON:	Mid-May through October
MAPS:	USGS 7.5 Frisco TI Vail/Frisco/Dillon

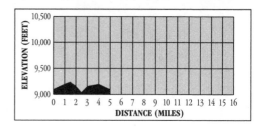

Crown Point Road, perfect for beginners and families, ends at a sandy beach on Lake Dillon that's ideal for picnics. Miles of abandoned road branch off the main route, accessing hours of exploring for riders of all abilities.

ACCESS: Drive south on HWY 9 just beyond Frisco. Turn left at the Peninsula Recreation Area (or Frisco Nordic Center) sign. Park immediately on the left just before a gate.

DESCRIPTION: Pedal through the gate and follow the main paved road past a group campground, restrooms and parking area on the right. Take the right fork of a paved road up a small hill and veer right onto a dirt road at a 3-way junction. Begin riding up this dirt road which leads to Crown Point. Go around a gate that remains closed in the summer to keep out motor vehicles. Follow this smooth, gently climbing route past many roads forking left and right. Some are marked by blue diamonds indicating their use as cross country ski trails during winter. Any of these spurs offer great exploring. This area is great for perfecting off-road skills. After reaching the high point, the road descends toward the lake and dead ends at a turnaround loop. At the beginning of the turnaround, turn right onto a faint trail that winds down to the beach. Sweeping views of the Continental Divide enhance the eastern skyline. Return as you came, enjoying close-up views of Peaks 1 and 2 in the Ten Mile Range.

COMMENTS: Snow melts quickly from this area, creating good early season riding conditions. Spurs branching off the main road offer hours of exploring. Crown Point Road may eventually be re-routed as more recreational opportunities are added to the area.

Stunning views toward the Continental Divide from Crown Point.

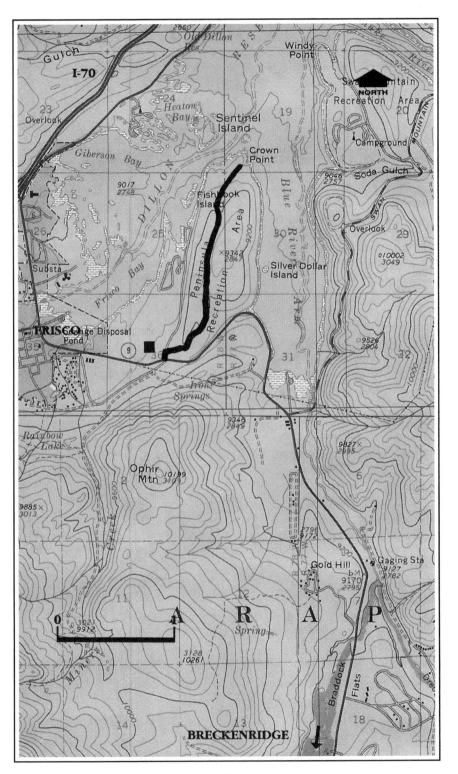

DISTANCE: 10.5 miles
TIME: 2-3 hours
RATING: Moderate-
more difficult*
ELEVATION: 9,040-10,260 ft.
GAIN: 1,220 ft.
TYPE: Loop;
trail/dirt rd./bike path
SEASON: Mid-June to mid-October
MAPS: USGS 7.5 Frisco
TI Vail/Frisco/Dillon

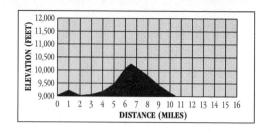

Gold Hill Trail is ideal for perfecting single track skills. This segment of the Colorado Trail travels over varied terrain and through scenery ranging from expansive meadows to dense lodgepole forests.

ACCESS: Drive south on HWY 9 just beyond Frisco. Turn right at signs for Rainbow Lake/Miner's Creek, (near Summit County government offices). Follow bike path signs and park in a pulloff on the left just before a gate.

DESCRIPTION: Ride up the bike path access. Cross the bikeway and follow a gravel road marked for Miner's Creek/Rainbow Lake. At the top of a small hill where the main road curves right, take a sharp left onto a route blocked to motorized traffic. Cruise through the trees, fork right at a junction and climb into a meadow dominated by views of Peak 1. At the southern end of the clearing, climb steeply through the trees. Drop into another clearing, pass the power line road and descend around a gate onto a gravel road. Turn right (the left turn enters private property) and drop onto the highway **(1.9 mi)**. Cross the highway and access the paved bike path. Follow it about 2.5 miles south toward Breckenridge. After crossing the highway again, look for Gold Hill trailhead at road #950 **(4.3 mi)**. The trail starts across from the parking area. The Ten Mile Range creates a striking backdrop as you climb through a beautiful sagebrush and wildflower-covered meadow. Rocky sections test your technical skills as the trail continues climbing. Cross the first of five abandoned logging roads **(5.3 mi)**. The trail continues on the other side. Cross another road and continue climbing on the trail, eventually connecting with a third road. Turn right on this road and follow it as it veers right, turns back into single track and continues ascending Gold Hill. Turn right at the next road. Pedal through a logged area and back into the trees where the route swings left, passing a spur on the right. A final technical climb brings you to the high point **(6.6 mi)**. The descent, rough at first, smooths out after crossing the last logging road and eventually connects with the Peaks Trail **(7.5 mi)**. (See ride 35.) Turn right onto the Peaks Trail and pedal north toward Frisco. An exhilarating descent brings you to Miner's Creek jeep road **(9.4 mi)**. Turn right onto the road and descend to the paved bike path, onto the access road and back to your vehicle.

COMMENTS: *Several rock-filled sections demand some technical skill. Expect other recreationalists on this popular trail, which is marked with blue diamonds the entire route. The northern end of this ride, near Miner's Creek/Rainbow Lake/Masontown region, is full of rideable jeep roads and trails.

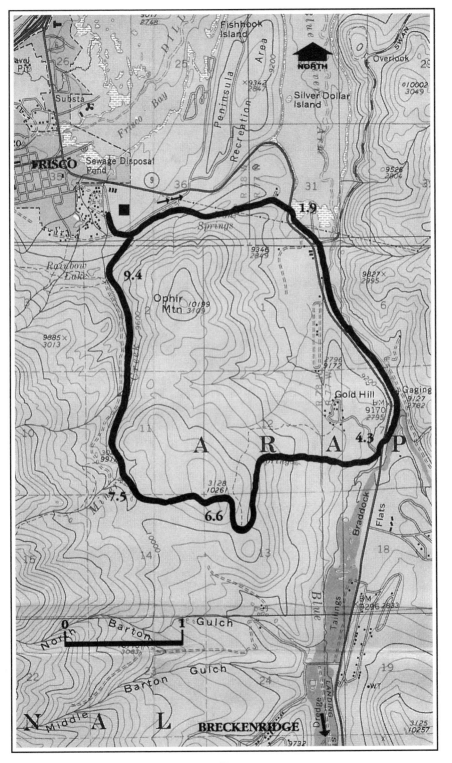

RIDE 35   PEAKS TRAIL

DISTANCE: 16 miles

TIME: 3-4 hours

RATING: Moderate*- more difficult

ELEVATION: 9,040-10,280 ft.

GAIN: 1,240 ft.

TYPE: Out&back; trail/dirt rd.

SEASON: Late June to mid-October

MAPS: USGS 7.5 Frisco-Breckenridge
TI Vail/Frisco/Dillon-Breckenridge South

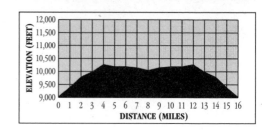

Connecting Frisco to Breckenridge, the popular Peaks Trail offers a variety of riding conditions on superb single track.

ACCESS: Drive south on HWY 9 just beyond Frisco. Turn right at signs for Rainbow Lake/Miner's Creek (near Summit County government offices). Follow bike path signs and park in a pulloff on the left just before a gate.

DESCRIPTION: Ride up the bike path access. Cross the bikeway and follow a gravel road marked for Miner's Creek/Rainbow Lake. Pedal along this road for roughly .8 miles as it climbs a small hill and winds through the trees. Look for the Peaks Trail forking left just before the road crosses the creek. Most of the elevation is gained in the first 3 miles as the trail climbs among the trees, past beaver ponds and along Miner's Creek. Pass the Gold Hill Trail **(2.8 mi)** (see ride 34) and continue straight until reaching Miner's Creek Trail **(3.1 mi)**. Veer left, staying on the Peaks Trail. The route levels a bit and passes by and through logged areas. At around **4.2 miles** begin following a water ditch off and on for the next mile. Creek crossings and tough technical sections have been eliminated by recent construction of log walkways that are very rideable. As you near Breckenridge the trail bisects a logging road, then crosses Cucumber Creek. Several more rocky sections keep you occupied until reaching the trailhead **(8.0 mi)**. Return as you came.

OPTION 1: To loop back on the paved bike path from the Breckenridge trailhead, turn right on the dirt road. Climb, then descend past the ski area and into Breckenridge. Access the bike path on the north end of town and follow it back to your vehicle. Total distance is increased by 3 miles.

OPTION 2: Park at the Breckenridge trailhead (beyond Peak 8 ski area on road #3), ride the trail down to Frisco and return to Breckenridge via the paved bike path. Most of the elevation gain is shifted to the gentle grade of the bike path. The only real climb is back to the trailhead and your vehicle. Total distance is increased by 3 miles.

OPTION 3: Using a shuttle vehicle and starting from the Breckenridge trailhead cuts the riding distance in half and drops this mainly downhill option to a moderate rating.

COMMENTS: *The majority of this ride is moderate although there are several short technical sections. Expect use by hikers and horsemen and anticipate heavy bike traffic on weekends. Stay on the designated route and walk around all muddy areas to preserve this recently improved trail. Blue markers attached to trees identify this path.

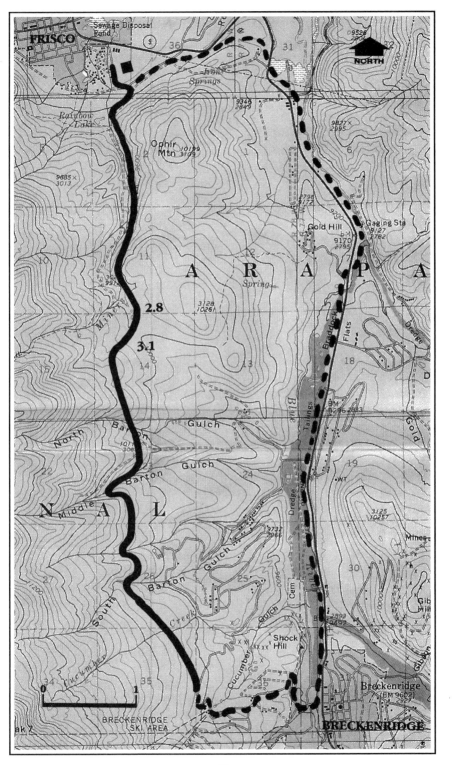

RIDE 36 MAYFLOWER GULCH

DISTANCE: 7 miles
TIME: 1-2 hours
RATING: Moderate
ELEVATION: 10,880-11,880 ft.
GAIN: 1,000 ft.
TYPE: Out&back;
dirt rd.
SEASON: Late June to early October
MAPS: USGS 7.5 Copper Mtn.
TI Breckenridge South

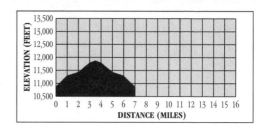

A well maintained jeep road provides access to a beautiful mountain cirque dotted with cabins, mining relics and fields of wildflowers.

ACCESS: Drive west on I-70 taking exit 195 for Copper Mountain. Drive toward Leadville on HWY 91 for 5.8 miles. Turn left and park in the Mayflower Gulch trailhead parking area.

DESCRIPTION: Follow the dirt road at the end of the parking lot. Stay on the roadway; at this point the surrounding land is private. Take the right fork and begin a steady 3.5-mile climb along the right side of the gulch. After an initial thigh-burning hill, this smooth dirt road alternates between short climbs and level recovery sections. After about a mile of pedaling, you pass an abandoned cabin and nearby ore chute. At timberline the road passes a fork on the right (see option). Continue through a gate and into a spectacular natural amphitheater. Ride past a group of cabins. Some are maintained for backcountry use; please help preserve them. The road climbs through high alpine vegetation, veers left and reaches a gate. Due to a small mining operation the route is closed beyond this point. Perched on the steep slopes above are remains of the Golden Crest Mine, in operation until the 1930's. The crumbling buildings in this wildflower-covered meadow are part of the abandoned townsite of Boston, at one time a successful mining community. Return as you came.

OPTION: Strong riders can lengthen the ride by following a side road starting near the gate for .6 miles to a tundra-covered ridge. Sweeping views into the Sawatch Range make the steep ascent worthwhile.

COMMENTS: Be prepared for exposure and weather changes; the last section of this ride climbs above timberline. Respect all private property near the beginning and end of this ride.

Remains of the Boston townsite in Mayflower Gulch.

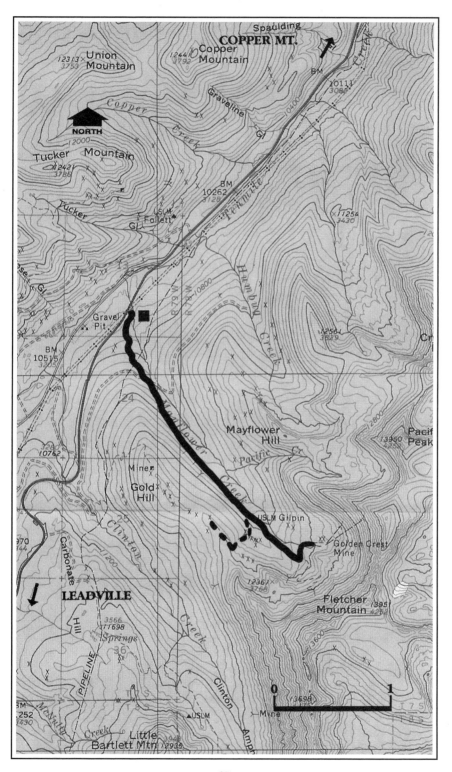

DISTANCE:	8.5 miles
TIME:	1-2 hours
RATING:	Easy*- moderate
ELEVATION:	9,677-10,320 ft.
GAIN:	643 ft.
TYPE:	Out&back; trail/dirt rd.
SEASON:	Mid-June to mid-October
MAPS:	USGS 7.5 Vail Pass-Copper Mtn. TI Vail/Frisco/Dillon-Breckenridge South

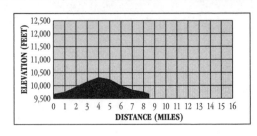

This abandoned railroad bed follows a gentle grade as it winds along Ten Mile Creek. Stream crossings and some rocky sections provide opportunities to practice technical skills.

ACCESS: Drive west on I-70, taking exit 195 at Copper Mountain. Turn left toward the gas station, and drive past it to the road's dead end at Wheeler Flats trailhead parking lot.

DESCRIPTION: Get on the paved bike path and cross a bridge. Turn right onto the Wheeler Trail (at this point a road) and cross another bridge. Follow this dirt road as it climbs parallel to HWY 91 through an open area that once supported the homestead of Judge Wheeler and the Wheeler townsite, which was eventually destroyed by fire. Wind along the left side of Ten Mile Creek, reaching the Wheeler Trail junction (see ride 7) and a bridge **(1.0 mi)**. Continue straight and cross the first of several streams that bisect the route. The road narrows to a trail and follows an old railroad grade, originally a flourishing railway corridor which provided much needed transportation from Frisco to Leadville. After walking around a grassy bog and crossing several more streams, you pass a weathered

cabin **(2.5 mi)**. Further up this drainage the trail widens to a road and passes a fork **(3.5 mi)** which descends to the creek. Continue straight, cross more streams and eventually connect with HWY 91 (see option). Return as you came.

OPTION: To loop this ride, return along HWY 91.

COMMENTS: *Ideal for beginning trail riders, this route has several technical stream crossings but remains an easy pedal. Riding conditions improve once the streams pass their peak runoff.

A meandering trail follows the abandoned railroad grade through Ten Mile Canyon.

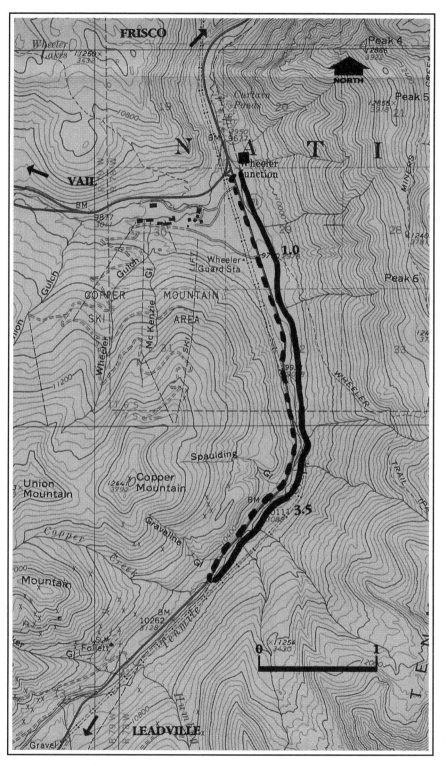

RIDE 38   SEARLE/KOKOMO PASSES

DISTANCE: 17.5 miles
TIME: 4-5 hours
RATING: More difficult
ELEVATION: 9,877-12,320 ft.
GAIN: 2,443 ft.
TYPE: Out&back; trail/bike path
SEASON: July through September
MAPS: USGS 7.5 Vail Pass-Copper Mtn. TI Breckenridge South-Vail/Frisco/Dillon

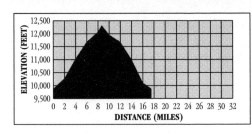

Following a section of the Colorado Trail, this superb single track winds up the side of a willow-filled valley onto tundra-covered slopes of two high alpine passes.

ACCESS: Drive west on I-70 taking exit 195 for Copper Mountain. Turn right at Copper Road and follow it through the resort. Turn right at Beeler Place and drive to the Union Creek parking lot.

DESCRIPTION: Access the paved bike path just beyond the parking lot near the stables. Follow it up West Ten Mile Creek for roughly **.9 miles**. Turn left and cross the bridge at the Colorado Trail sign. The trail swings left, crosses under the Interstate and over Guller Creek. Occasional horse/nordic trails merge from the left as you climb along the right side of the drainage. A combination of technical sections, creek crossings and moderate climbs provide plenty of variety. Pass a collapsed cabin and horse trail (closed to bikes) on the left **(2.2 mi)**. Soon the drainage widens, providing sweeping views to Elk Ridge. Tough-to-spot remains of several cabins dot the trail's edge. Climb through a series of switchbacks to timberline where you'll see Searle Pass between Jacque Ridge and Elk Mountain. Curve left at the head of the drainage and look below for a glimpse of Janet's Cabin (open during winter on a reservation basis). Switchback upward through the tundra. Remain on the designated route to avoid damaging the fragile vegetation. Reach Searle Pass after a final rocky pitch (expect to walk) **(6.5 mi)**. This is a good turning around point for those short on time, energy or clear skies. The trail veers right on the other side of the pass. Entirely above timberline but well marked by large cairns, it climbs gradually along Elk Ridge. Several switchbacks bring you to the high point. Mountain ranges too numerous to identify dominate the skyline and the Climax settling ponds (which obliterated several mining communities) cover the valley floor. The ride ends here since Kokomo Pass is actually below this point. (See ride 39.) Return as you came.

OPTION: Adventurous riders can loop this trip by picking their way down the other side of Searle Pass. A faint trail leads to a double track which drops to a well traveled dirt road. Turn left at this road, pass through a gate and descend around the edge of mining operations until joining HWY 91. Follow the highway down to Copper Mountain and loop back to your vehicle.

COMMENTS: Expect hiking and horse traffic. Avoid this trail after significant rainfalls. Much of this ride is above timberline; be prepared for changing weather conditions.

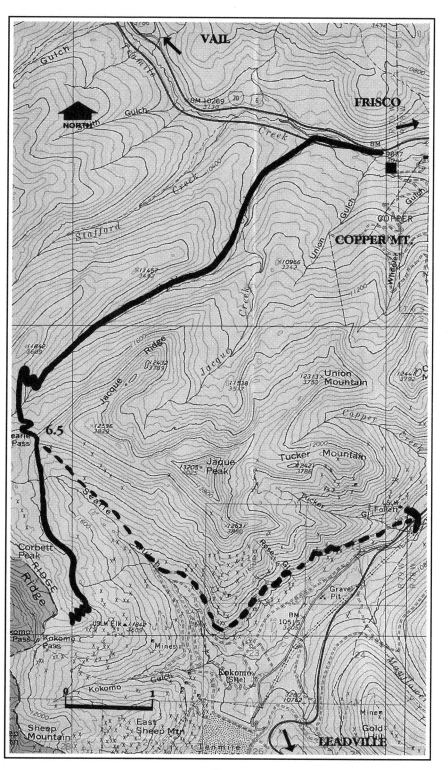

RIDE 39 OVER ELK RIDGE

DISTANCE: 29 miles
TIME: 7-8 hours
RATING: Advanced
ELEVATION: 9,240-12,320 ft.
GAIN: 3,080 ft.
TYPE: Loop;
trail/dirt rd./bike path
SEASON: July through September
MAPS: USGS 7.5 Vail Pass-Copper Mtn.-Pando-Redcliff
TI Breckenridge South-Vail/Frisco/Dillon

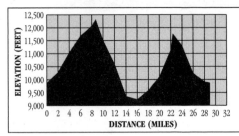

An outstanding section of the Colorado Trail, miles of above timberline ped-aling and varied scenery combine to create a challenging but rewarding loop.

ACCESS: Drive west on I-70 taking exit 195 for Copper Mountain. Turn right at Copper Road and follow it through the resort. Turn right at Beeler Place and drive to the Union Creek parking lot.

DESCRIPTION: Access the paved bike path beyond the parking lot near the stables. Follow it up West Ten Mile Creek for roughly **.9 miles**. Turn left and cross a bridge at the Colorado Trail sign. The trail swings left, crosses under the Interstate and over Guller Creek. Ascending the right side of the drainage the route combines technical sections, creek crossings and moderate climbs. A horse trail forking left near cabin remains in a meadow is the only deceiving spur. Switchback up to timberline and swing left toward Searle Pass. Look for Janet's Cabin just below treeline (open during winter on a reservation basis). Reach Searle Pass after a final rocky pitch **(6.5 mi)**. The trail, marked by large cairns, veers right on the other side of the pass and climbs gradually through the tundra below Elk Ridge. Switchback up to the high point for endless views including numerous mountain ranges and large uninterrupted expanses of tundra. Descend to Kokomo Pass **(9.2 mi)** and drop right off the saddle for a screaming downhill into Camp Hale. The trail swoops into a deep drainage, turns to road, continues descending steeply, at times, and passes a couple faint spurs on the left. Cross Cataract Creek **(12.5 mi)** and at an intersection, continue on the route identified by Colorado Trail tree markers. Descend to the valley floor **(13.2 mi)**. Turn left at the junction and drop onto a main dirt road. Turn right and cruise along the edge of the valley. Nearly level and occasionally paved, this road passes many forks to the left and right as it travels the area where the 10th Mountain Division trained for World War II. Pedal for almost 4 miles until encountering two 3-way junctions. Stay right at both, cross over Resolution Creek and begin climbing Resolution Road #702. Easy at first, this ascent becomes strenuous and tiring for the last 2 miles but remains completely rideable. Stay on the main road at all spurs, including a deceptive turnoff (road #751) forking left just before the top. Crest Ptarmigan Pass **(22.4 mi)** and continue down the other side into the trees. Upon reaching an open area, look for an abandoned double track on the right **(23.2 mi)** where the main road drops left into Wearyman Gulch. (See ride 41.) Take the less-used route, forking right onto a faint road blocked by logs. Descend along the left side of Wilder Gulch. Alternating single and double track crosses streams and bogs before passing under I-70 and connecting with the paved bike path **(25.5 mi)**. Turn right onto the bikeway and descend for roughly 3.6 miles to your vehicle.

COMMENTS: A glance at the hill profile confirms this loop's difficulty. Strong physical condition, plenty of food and water and guaranteed good weather are a necessity. Expect hikers and horsemen on the Colorado Trail which becomes a mess after heavy rains and should be avoided. You may encounter traffic in Camp Hale and on Resolution Road.

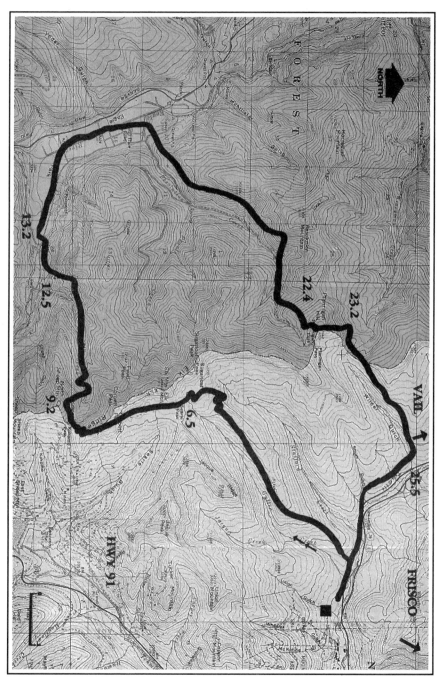

RIDE 40 WILDER GULCH

DISTANCE: 9 miles
TIME: 2-3 hours
RATING: Moderate-more difficult
ELEVATION: 10,500-11,765 ft.
GAIN: 1,265 ft.
TYPE: Out&back; trail/dirt rd./bike path
SEASON: Late June to early October
MAPS: USGS 7.5 Vail Pass-Redcliff-Pando
TI Breckenridge South-Vail/Frisco/Dillon

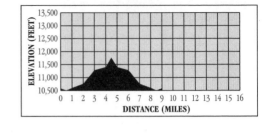

The Wilder Gulch ride climbs gradually through a large meadow, crossing many small streams and bogs. Tundra-covered Ptarmigan Pass, with its endless vistas, is the final destination.

ACCESS: Drive west on I-70 to Vail Pass. Turn off at exit 190, cross over the Interstate and park at the rest area.

DESCRIPTION: Descend a little over **.5 miles** on the paved bike path as it heads toward Copper Mountain. After a series of curves look for a gray electrical box in a clump of trees on the right. Turn here onto a faint trail. Ride under the Interstate. Climb a small hill on the right, curve left and ride up the right side of Wilder Gulch along an old road that has reverted back to single track. After a couple of short, steep, technical climbs the gulch widens into a large meadow. For the next couple of miles wet, boggy areas and stream crossings alternate with dry single track. Portage any muddy areas to avoid leaving ruts. The trail eventually becomes a faint road which climbs into the trees. It veers right, passes through a meadow and merges with a major dirt road **(3.5 mi)**. The right fork drops into Wearyman Gulch. (See ride 41.) For this ride turn left, climb through the forest and above timberline to Ptarmigan Pass. Panoramic views in all directions make the ascent worthwhile**.** The road continues down to Camp Hale. From the pass, return as you came.

OPTION: Wilder Gulch can be accessed from Copper Mountain by riding roughly 3.6 miles up the paved bike path.

COMMENTS: This ride becomes easier during mid-summer once spring runoff subsides. The pass is above timberline; be prepared for changing weather conditions.

High above timberline on Ptarmigan Pass.

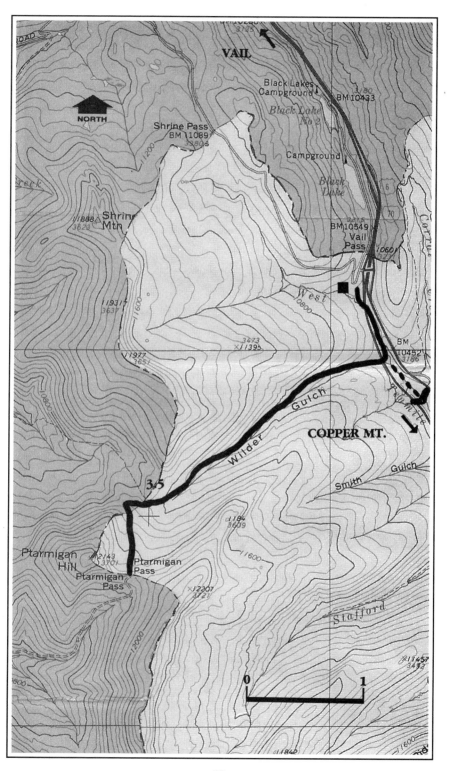

VAIL

Black Lakes
Campground
BM 10433

Black Lake
No 2

Campground

Black Lake

NORTH

Shrine Pass
BM 11089

Shrine
Mth

BM 10549
Vail
Pass

West

BM
10452

Wilder   Gulch

COPPER MT.

Gulch

Smith

3.5

Ptarmigan
Hill

Ptarmigan
Pass

Ptarmigan
Pass

Stafford

0   1

93

RIDE 41   AROUND SHRINE MOUNTAIN

DISTANCE: 17 miles

TIME: 4-5 hours

RATING: Moderate-more difficult

ELEVATION: 9,000-11,400 ft.

GAIN: 2,400 ft.

TYPE: Loop; trail/dirt rd.

SEASON: Late June to early October

MAPS: USGS 7.5 Vail Pass-Redcliff
TI Vail/Frisco/Dillon

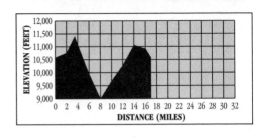

Exploring mountains west of Vail Pass, this ride combines varied terrain in Wilder and Wearyman Gulches with the aspen-lined beauty of Shrine Pass Road.

ACCESS: Drive west on I-70 to Vail Pass. Turn off at exit 190, cross over the Interstate and park at the rest area.

DESCRIPTION: Descend a little over **.5 miles** on the paved bike path as it heads toward Copper Mountain. After a series of curves look for a gray electrical box in a clump of trees on the right. Turn here onto a faint trail. Ride under the Interstate. Climb a small hill on the right, curve left and ride up the right side of Wilder Gulch along an old road that has reverted back to trail. After a couple of short, steep, technical climbs the gulch widens into a large meadow. For the next couple of miles wet, boggy areas and stream crossings alternate with dry single track. Portage any muddy areas to avoid leaving ruts. The trail eventually becomes a faint road which climbs into the trees. It veers right, passes through a meadow and merges with a major dirt road **(3.5 mi)**. Turn right onto this road (see ride 40 to continue up Wilder Gulch) and begin a 4.5-mile descent through Wearyman Gulch. The route leaves the trees and spills onto grassy slopes. Alternating smooth and rocky terrain punctuated with occasional stream crossings creates a fun and varied descent. At about **7.0 miles** you reach the first of several major stream crossings that can be either ridden or waded. At a 3-way junction follow the right fork, which crosses a bridge and descends along the right side of the gulch. The stream fords come in quick succession until merging with Shrine Pass Road **(8.0 mi)**. Turn right (a left turn leads to Redcliff-see option) onto this smooth dirt road and begin a moderate 7-mile climb to Shrine Pass. Starting along the banks of Turkey Creek and eventually crossing to green hillsides above the left side of the streambed, the route passes spurs, roofless cabins, a rest area and the side road to Shrine Mountain Inn before reaching the pass. Stay in the main drainage on road #709 at any junctions. A refreshing 1.5-mile descent brings you to Vail Pass and your vehicle.

OPTION: The final 7-mile climb can be eliminated by turning left onto Shrine Pass Road and descending about 2.5 miles to a shuttle vehicle which has been left in Redcliff.

COMMENTS: Expect heavy traffic on Shrine Pass Road during weekends. An abundance of aspen make this a great fall ride. Plan on getting your feet wet during the many crossings of Wearyman Creek. Shrine Mountain Inn (303-476-6548) offers dining and overnight accommodations.

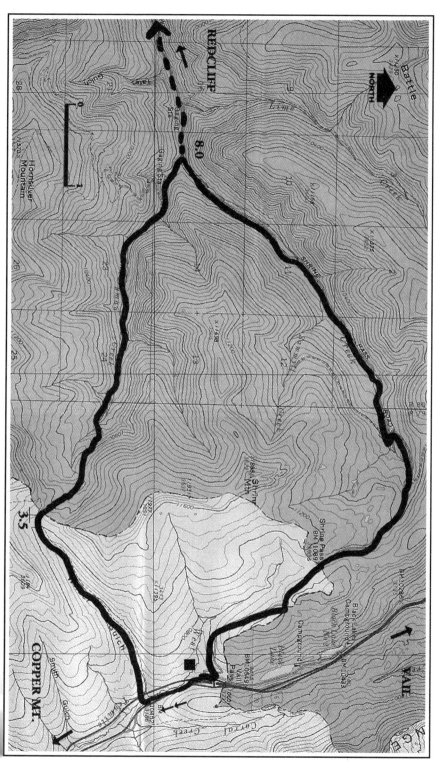

RIDE 42   LIME CREEK

DISTANCE: 22.5 miles

TIME: 4-5 hours

RATING: Easy*- more difficult

ELEVATION: 8,900-11,200 ft.

GAIN: 2,300 ft.

TYPE: Loop; dirt rd.

SEASON: Late June to early October

MAPS: USGS 7.5 Vail Pass-Redcliff
TI Vail/Frisco/Dillon

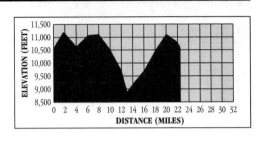

A thorough exploration of the Shrine Pass area and its extreme terrain contrasts, ranging from high alpine meadows to steeply walled drainages, are highlights of the Lime Creek loop.

ACCESS: Drive west on I-70 to Vail Pass. Turn off at exit 190, cross over the Interstate and park in the rest area.

DESCRIPTION: Follow the dirt road for Shrine Pass/Redcliff that climbs above the parking lot. Ascend gradually along this well maintained route to the high point **(1.7 mi)**. Descend, passing the Shrine Mountain Inn access road and a scenic viewpoint. Reach a major 3-way junction **(4.0 mi)** and turn right onto Lime Creek Road #728. Turn left at the next junction, remaining on road #728. Begin several miles of contouring along the south side of a ridge on this smooth dirt road. Rolling terrain and occasional glimpses into the Holy Cross Wilderness characterize the riding. A pullout on the left near a gated road **(8.0 mi)** offers unlimited views to the southwest. (The easy pedaling ends here-see option 1.) Descend on the main road which narrows considerably after one mile. SLOW DOWN as the road switchbacks left and look for a side road dropping steeply to the right. (You've missed it if you pass through a green gate onto a logging road.) Turn onto this rough jeep track and drop to Lime Creek **(9.3 mi)**. Hemmed in by the grassy slopes of Battle Mountain on the right and dense forest on the left, a rarely-used double track drops steeply along lush green hillsides. Some technical skill is needed to negotiate rough sections that break up an otherwise smooth descent. Huge walls of aspen line the lower slopes, offering a multi-colored treat during fall. After crossing the creek, the pitch steepens, containing a couple of particularly rough sections that may require walking. Turn left upon reaching Shrine Pass Road **(13 mi)**. (A right turn leads to Redcliff-see option 2.) Begin a moderate 7-mile climb to Shrine Pass. Starting on the banks of Turkey Creek and eventually crossing to green hillsides above the left side of the streambed, the route passes several major side roads and many campsite spurs. Stay in the main drainage on road #709 at any junctions. Pass the familiar Lime Creek turnoff, backtrack over Shrine Pass and down to your vehicle.

OPTION 1: Novices may want to return as they came from the viewpoint. This 16-mile out and back ride eliminates a technical descent and 7 miles of climbing.

OPTION 2: The final 7-mile climb can be avoided by turning right onto Shrine Pass Road and descending roughly 2 miles to a shuttle vehicle which has been left in Redcliff.

COMMENTS: *The first 8 miles are easy pedaling. Expect heavy traffic on Shrine Pass Road during weekends. Shrine Mountain Inn (303-476-6548) offers dining and overnight accommodations.

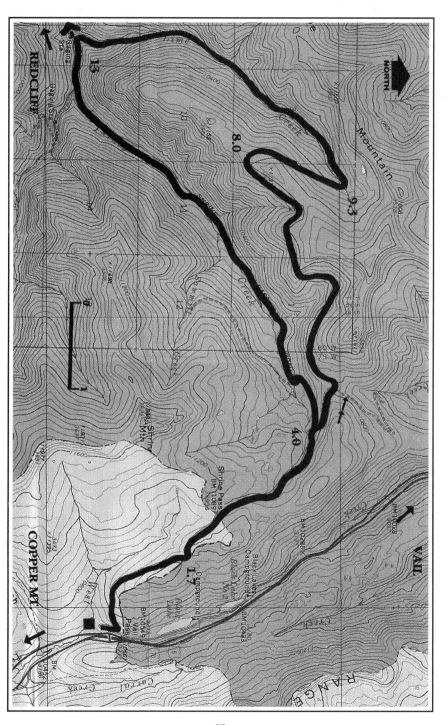

RIDE 43   TWO ELK TRAIL

DISTANCE: 18 miles

TIME: 5 hours

RATING: More difficult-advanced*

ELEVATION: 9,200-11,696 ft.

GAIN: 2,496 ft.

TYPE: Loop; trail/dirt rd./bike path

SEASON: July to early October

MAPS: USGS 7.5 Vail Pass-Redcliff TI Vail/Frisco/Dillon

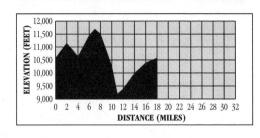

Stunning views into the Gore Range and 7 miles of fast-paced trail highlight this fantastic loop which tours old growth forests and exposed ridges west of Vail Pass.

ACCESS: Drive west on I-70 to Vail Pass. Turn off at exit 190, cross over the Interstate and park in the rest area.

DESCRIPTION: Follow the dirt road for Shrine Pass/Redcliff that climbs above the parking lot. Ascend gradually along this well maintained route to the high point **(1.7 mi)**. Descend, passing the Shrine Mountain Inn access road and a scenic viewpoint. Reach a major 3-way junction **(4.0 mi)** and turn right onto Lime Creek Road #728. Curve left and climb, passing a spur on the right. A short distance later the signed Two Elk trailhead appears on the right. (See ride 42 for a continuation of Lime Creek Road.) Turn onto the single track and climb into the trees. This ultra-smooth trail (called Bowman's Cutoff) snakes its way up onto a ridge. Several steep switchbacks challenge even the strongest pedalers but most of the route climbs moderately. Swinging back and forth between one side of the ridge and the other, riders are blasted with close-up views into the Gore Range and distant southwestern ranges. Reach the top of the first of several knolls **(6.2 mi)**. Drop just a little, then climb onto an open ridge where views into Holy Cross Wilderness dominate. The trail becomes faint as it swings right, then left and meanders along a grassy slope. Reach a sign/cairn **(7.2 mi)** and yet another gorgeous view. Drop, steeply at first, off the back side of this knoll into a dense forest full of massive old growth trees. After a final climb, descend steeply over root and rock-filled terrain. Reach a signed trail junction on the wooded Two Elk Pass **(8.8 mi)**. Turn sharply right onto the trail descending to I-70. (The left fork continues to Minturn-see option.) Disappearing through a heavily wooded hillside, the trail plummets downward. Steep dropoffs and challenging switchbacks dictate the need for caution. Soon the trail gradient mellows but still contains several technical, eroded areas that may need to be walked around. Bridge crossings indicate the descent's end. Ride under the Interstate, climb briefly and connect with a paved road **(11.2 mi)**. Turn right and ascend on the Vail Pass/Ten Mile Canyon National Recreation Trail (at this point a road). Veer right about a mile later at the sign for "Recreation Trail" which is the actual bike path. Continue climbing for another 5.3 miles until reaching Vail Pass and your vehicle.

OPTION: Skilled riders can further explore Two Elk Trail by turning left from the pass and descending 6.5 miles to a trailhead 2 miles south of Minturn on HWY 24 where a shuttle vehicle is waiting.

COMMENTS: *Several descents are steep, technical, pass near intimidating dropoffs and require solid technical skills. Avoid this ride after heavy rains. Expect traffic on Shrine Pass Road and hikers on the trail.

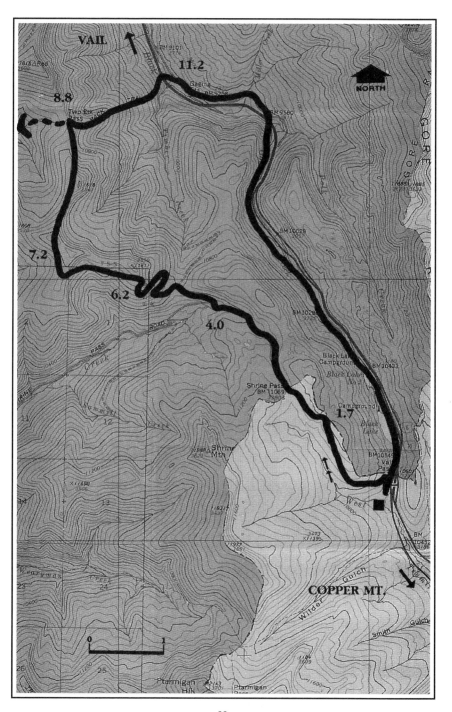

RIDE 44   PTARMIGAN PEAK

DISTANCE: 12 miles
TIME: 5 hours
RATING: Advanced
ELEVATION: 9,040-12,498 ft.
GAIN: 3,458 ft.
TYPE: Out&back; trail
SEASON: July through September
MAPS: USGS 7.5 Dillon
TI Vail/Frisco/Dillon

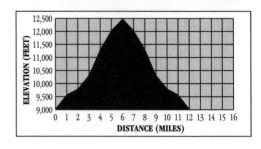

The tundra-covered summit of Ptarmigan Peak, reached by a challenging single track ascent, offers some of the most expansive views in Summit County.

ACCESS: From I-70 take exit #205 at Silverthorne and turn north onto HWY 9. Turn right at the stoplight by Wendy's. Follow Tanglewood Lane which veers right, passing restaurants and hotels. Turn right at the stop sign onto road #2021. Fork right at the junction, remaining on #2021 which becomes dirt and climbs to trailhead parking on the right.

DESCRIPTION: The trail, which begins opposite the parking area, starts climbing immediately. After connecting with a road for a short distance it forks right onto a sagebrush-covered hillside and begins a brutal climb around the side of a small knoll. This first segment of trail travels through private land; stay on the designated route. After merging with an old road, climb further; then drop into an aspen grove and cross another double track. The trail continues on the other side. Starting out gradually, this buffed path winds through lush stands of aspen and contours north along the lower slopes of the peak. Glimpses across the valley to the Gore Range and south to Lake Dillon give you an idea of the striking views gained from the top. As you switchback up into the pines, the gradient becomes steeper and the terrain more rocky. However, the trail remains completely rideable the entire distance. The transition to timberline is marked by fields of lupine and paintbrush wildflowers. Leave the forest behind and merge with a faint road **(4.3 mi)**. Turn left and follow this road through rolling slopes of high alpine tundra toward a cairn marked with a stake. The summit is finally reached after roughly 1.5 miles of strenuous pedaling over a couple of false summits. Stunning views and a top-of-the-world feeling make the effort worthwhile. The descent is another well-earned reward but can go too quickly. Take your time and control your speed; hikers and horsemen also use this trail. (DO NOT miss the right turn onto the trail at timberline; the road also descends to the bottom but *is not* recommended!)

COMMENTS: This route is a popular hunting access in the fall. Choose a guaranteed good-weather day to ride; you're above timberline for a long time. Protect fragile tundra by staying on the trail.

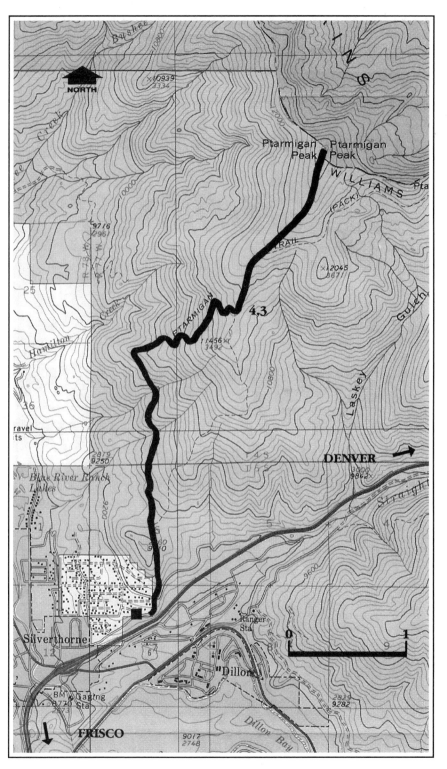

DISTANCE:	21 miles
TIME:	4 hours
RATING:	Moderate
ELEVATION:	10,250-11,200 ft.
GAIN:	950 ft.
TYPE:	Out&back; dirt rd.
SEASON:	Late June to early October
MAPS:	USGS 7.5 King Creek-Battle Mtn.-Squaw Creek TI Green Mtn. Reservoir/Ute Pass

This rolling ridgetop ride along the Williams Fork Range follows a jeep road over terrain containing minimal elevation changes. Numerous viewpoints provide breathtaking vistas of the Gore Range and into Williams Fork drainage.

ACCESS: Drive 25 miles north of Silverthorne on HWY 9, passing Green Mountain Reservoir. Turn right onto Williams Peak Road and follow it for 6 miles to the ridgetop. Park at the 3-way junction.

DESCRIPTION: Begin riding south on road #200, which forks right from the 3-way junction. The first two miles consist of great cruising along grassy slopes and through aspen groves. On calm days you may see hangliders; the ridge is a favorite launching site. At almost **2.5 miles** begin a steady, one-mile climb that takes you higher onto the ridge. The road then levels and winds through the cool shade of the trees. Pass a couple of side roads, the first drops steeply to the left while another forks right a short distance further. Beyond the second spur begin contouring around the left side of Williams Peak over a rocky section of road. After rounding the peak, pass another spur which drops off to the left. Beyond this point you are treated to the first of several spectacular viewpoints. The rugged Gore Range fills the entire western horizon. Continue winding along the ridge through dense forests and past exposed viewpoints. While contouring along northeast slopes, you pass a trailhead for Williams Peak Trail on the left **(8.5 mi)**. Continue on the road past another viewpoint, veer left and descend gradually to the route's dead end on the north side of Prairie Mountain **(10.5 mi)**. Return as you came.

COMMENTS: This route is easily shortened by turning around at one of the viewpoints. Expect hunting traffic during fall.

The Gore Range provides a breathtaking backdrop along Williams Fork Road.

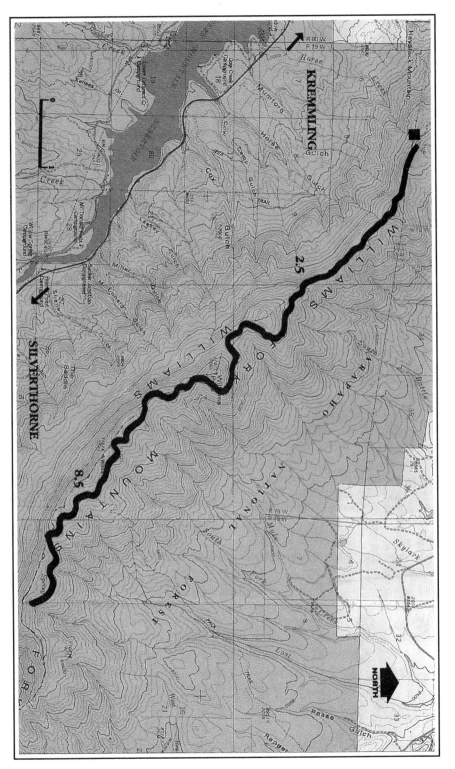

DISTANCE: 10.5 miles

TIME: 2 hours

RATING: Easy*-moderate

ELEVATION: 8,650-9,670 ft.

GAIN: 1,020 ft.

TYPE: Out&back; dirt rd.

SEASON: June through October

MAPS: USGS 7.5 Sheephorn Mtn.
TI Green Mtn. Reservoir/Ute Pass

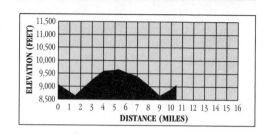

Heading south along the foothills of the Gore Range, this well maintained road offers sweeping views both east towards the Continental Divide and west into the Flat Tops Wilderness.

ACCESS: Drive 26 miles north of Silverthorne on HWY 9, passing Green Mountain Reservoir. Turn left onto Spring Creek Road. Follow this dirt road as it crosses the Blue River, switchbacks up and across a cattle guard at 5.2 miles. At 5.8 miles cross a second cattle guard and park on the left at a 3-way junction.

DESCRIPTION: Follow the right fork which heads north toward Dice Hill. Descend for the first mile through an idyllic aspen-fringed meadow. Unobstructed views to the east reveal several massive mountain ranges. The road swings left and begins a moderate 2-mile climb back onto National Forest land. A smooth road surface and cool shade from the trees help this ascent go quickly. Climbing to the west and around the side of Dice Hill you catch glimpses of the Flat Tops Wilderness. The road levels and contours along the western slope of Dice Hill. After another shorter climb you reach a turnaround. A less-traveled road veers right along a fence. Follow this road a short distance to the high point and choose from the many log perches for a chance to sit and gaze at the 360 degree view. Mt Powell, the northernmost peak in the Gore Range, dominates the southern horizon. The road continues down into the trees but becomes less rideable. From the high point, return as you came.

COMMENTS: *This ride contains no technical challenges but does have a sustained, moderate climb of 2 miles. Private property surrounds the first 1.5 miles of road; stay on the described route. This is a beautiful fall ride, but be aware of hunters who frequent the area.

Easy cruising on the road to Dice Hill.

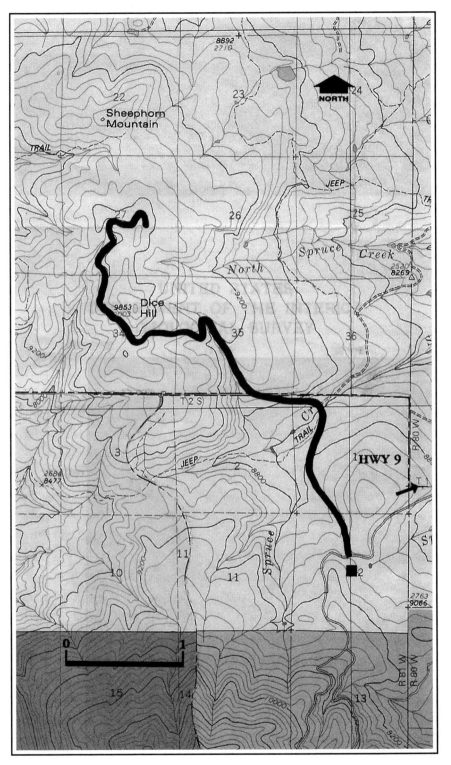

RIDE 47   MAHAN LAKE

DISTANCE: 12 miles
TIME: 3 hours
RATING: Moderate*-
more difficult
ELEVATION: 10,050-11,200 ft.
GAIN: 1,150 ft.
TYPE: Loop;
dirt rd.
SEASON: Late June to early October
MAPS: USGS 7.5 Piney Peak
TI Green Mtn. Reservoir/Ute Pass

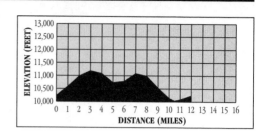

Roads crisscrossing the northern Gore Range provide a variety of riding conditions. This route traverses meadows along Elliot Ridge and winds through dense forests. A short side trip leads to secluded Mahan Lake.

ACCESS: Drive 26 miles north of Silverthorne on HWY 9, passing Green Mountain Reservoir. Turn left onto Spring Creek Road. Follow this dirt road as it crosses the Blue River, switchbacks up and across a cattleguard at 5.2 miles. Beyond a second cattleguard near a junction, take the left fork. Turn left again at a sign for Sheephorn Divide/Mahan Lake. Drive 3.4 miles and park at a spur marked by a sign for End of Road/Mahan Lake.

DESCRIPTION: From the junction, ride up the right fork toward Mahan Lake. Pedal through a gate and climb moderately for about 1.5 miles past several side roads. Turn left at a 3-way junction on the ridgetop. Climb gradually along the ridge to a junction signed for Mahan Lake/Elliot Ridge **(2.5 mi)**. Turn left toward the lake and descend into the trees. Pass road #281 on the left **(3.5 mi)** (you'll return to this junction to complete the loop) and continue straight, climbing out of the trees and into lush meadows below Elliot Ridge. Wind along below the ridge heading south toward massive Mt. Powell. The more difficult part of this ride begins as the road veers away from the ridge and drops steeply. (Less skilled riders may want to turn around here and return to the loop section of the ride.) Descend for roughly .5 miles to a junction. An abandoned road, marked as the Gore Range Trail (impassable due to fallen timber), forks left **(5.0 mi)**. The right fork continues to Mahan Lake. It climbs over rougher terrain for about .6 miles, passing a fork to the left and later, another to the right, before dropping to a stream. Turn right beyond the stream and pedal up to the tree-rimmed lake. To complete the loop, backtrack for 1.7 miles to the junction with road #281. Turn right onto #281 and descend into the trees, staying on the main route where a side road forks right. Stay right at the next junction, continuing on #281. Descend for roughly 1.8 miles through forested and open areas. (Since this area was once logged, you'll pass many abandoned side roads.) Follow the main route until connecting with a well-traveled road **(9.8 mi)**. Turn left and ride for another 2 miles until reaching your vehicle.

COMMENTS: *Except for the exploration to Mahan Lake, this is a moderate ride. Numerous spur roads make the last 4 miles of this ride a navigational challenge. Miles of roads crisscross this region making it an ideal area to camp and spend a few days exploring. Hunters frequent this area in the fall. A proposed timber cut may cause route changes in upcoming years.

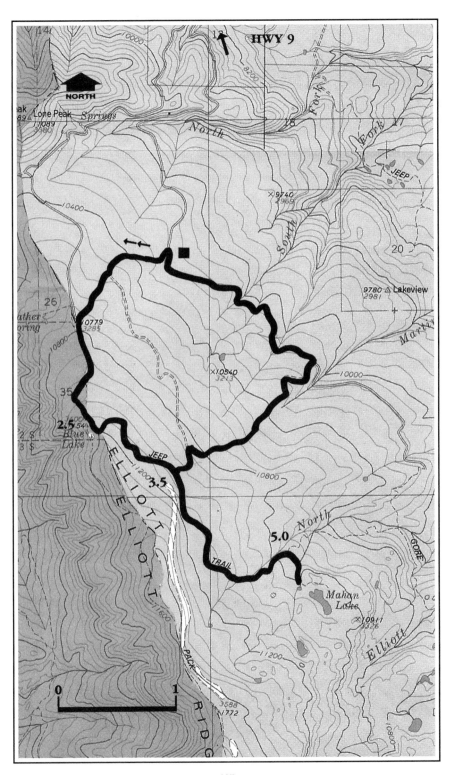

Summit County – Trailhead Locations

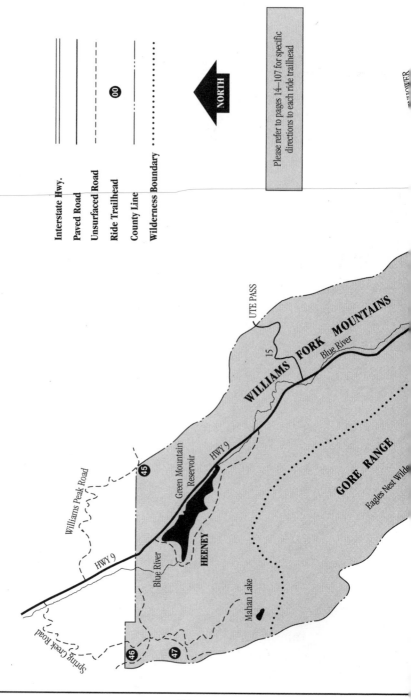

Interstate Hwy.

Paved Road

Unsurfaced Road

Ride Trailhead 00

County Line

Wilderness Boundary

NORTH

Please refer to pages 14–107 for specific directions to each ride trailhead

UTE PASS

WILLIAMS FORK MOUNTAINS

Blue River

15

Williams Peak Road

45

Green Mountain Reservoir

HWY 9

HWY 9

Blue River

HEENEY

Spring Creek Road

46

47

Mahan Lake

GORE RANGE

Eagles Nest Wilde...

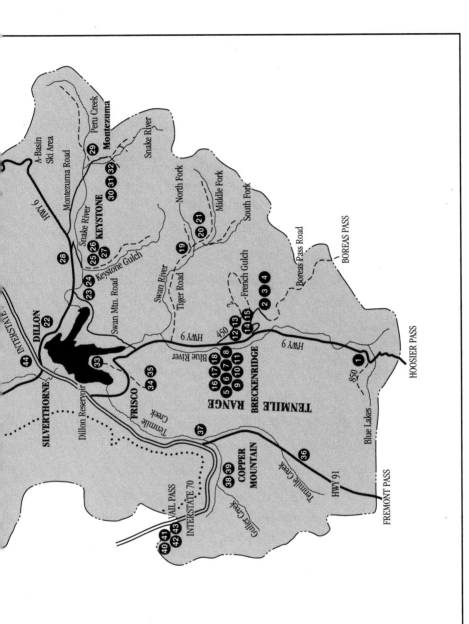

Rides By Difficulty

Easy

Boreas Pass, p. 16
Crown Point, p. 78

French Gulch, p. 36

Tenderfoot Rd., p. 56

Easy–moderate

Blue Lakes, p. 14
Preston, p. 44

Blue River Trail, p. 28
Ten Mile Canyon, p. 86

Sally Barber Mine, p. 38
Dice Hill, p. 104

Easy–more difficult

Keystone Gulch, p. 62

Lime Creek, p. 96

Easy–advanced

Three Forks of the Swan, p. 52

Moderate

Baker's Tank Loop, p. 18
Frey Gulch, p. 68

Boreas Pass Loop, p. 20
Mayflower Gulch, p. 84

Soda Creek, p. 58
Williams Fork Ridge, p. 102

Moderate–more difficult

Burro Trail-Spruce Crk., p. 22
Golden Horseshoe, p. 46
After-work Special, p. 60
Peru Creek, p. 70
Gold Hill, p. 80
Around Shrine Mt., p. 94

Pennsylvania-Indiana, p. 30
Gold Run, p. 48
West Ridge, p. 64
Hunkidori Mine, p. 72
Peaks Trail, p. 82
Mahan Lake, p. 106

Dyersville, p. 32
Swan River Loop, p. 50
Keystone Gulch-Soda Crk., p. 66
Webster Pass, p. 74
Wilder Gulch, p. 92

More Difficult

Fall Classic, p. 40

Searle/Kokomo Passes, p. 88

More difficult–advanced

Hoosier Ridge, p. 34
Two Elk Trail, p. 98

Around Mt. Guyot, p. 42

Georgia Pass, p. 54

Advanced

Wheeler Trail South, p. 24
Over Elk Ridge, p. 90

Wheeler Trail North, p. 26
Ptarmigan Peak, p. 100

Montezuma Loop, p. 76

Suggested Contacts

USFS-Dillon Ranger District
PO Box 620
Silverthorne, Colorado 80498
(303) 468-5400

Summit County Chamber of Commerce
PO Box 214
Frisco, Colorado 80443
(303) 668-5800

Breckenridge Resort Chamber
PO Box 1909
Breckenridge, Colorado 80424
(303) 453-5579 (303) 453-6018

Breckenridge Fat Tire Society
PO Box 2845
Breckenridge, Colorado 80424

Bicycle Colorado
PO Box 3877
Littleton, CO 80161
(303) 798-1429

International Mt. Bike Assoc. (IMBA)
PO Box 412043
Los Angeles, CA 90041
(818) 792-8830

Recommended Maps

U.S. Forest Service: Arapaho National Forest-Dillon Ranger District (covers all of Summit County), Arapaho National Forest (covers most of the rides), Pike National Forest (covers rides that continue south of the Continental Divide into Park County), White River National Forest (covers rides that continue west of the county line near Vail Pass)

Forest Service maps are available from the Dillon Ranger District office (see contacts).

USGS County Series: Summit County 1 & 2, Park County 1 (covers rides continuing south of the Continental Divide into Park County), Grand County 3 (covers rides continuing east and north of the Lower Blue River Valley), Eagle County 4 (covers rides continuing west of the county line near Vail Pass)

Topographic maps are available from the following Summit County retailers: Wilderness Sports, Daily Planet Bookstore, Weber's Books and Drawings, Knorr House.

For Your Information

Where did they go? Why some original routes are deleted from the second edition.
1. The Flume Ride: Much of this route crosses private land. The property owners no longer allow access onto the flume.
2. Mayflower Lake: The trail from Spruce Creek Road to Mayflower Lake is so eroded that it's no longer rideable.
3. Mahan Lake Connector: The road connecting Mahan Lake to the lower part of the loop is obstructed by fallen timber, making it more of a portage than a ride.

Listed below are future changes and additions that may occur on both private and public lands throughout Summit County. Several of these changes are development oriented and will affect biking routes and their access (i.e. closures and re-routings). Changes on National Forests include logging and mining operations that may temporarily alter ride descriptions.

1. Completion of the Colorado Trail between the North Fork of the Swan and HWY 9.
2. Re-routing and maintenance on the first section of the Blue River Trail, south of Breckenridge.
3. Possible addition of more mountain bike routes in the Peninsula Recreation Area, near Frisco.
4. A non-motorized route from Breckenridge onto Bald Mountain.
5. More development (residential, paved roads, etc.) in French Gulch, the Swan River Valley and up onto the ridge between the two.
6. Residential development near Summit Cove and Keystone Ranch.
7. Who knows? Anticipate anything!

Get involved! If you want help with new trail construction, have ideas on potential bike routes, are displeased with a logging operation, concerned with a trail closure or upset about a development project...ACT! Contact one of the groups or individuals listed below.

1. Breckenridge Fat Tire Society (deals with land access issues, trail maintenance, new routes-see contacts)
2. U. S. Forest Service (deals with land trades, logging operations, misuse of public lands-see contacts)
3. Summit County Commissioners (vocalize or mail your concerns to them)
4. Local newspapers (a letter to the editor is an excellent way to get your message to the public)

Keep this book updated. All of the information in this guide was accurate as of fall, 1992. However, changes do occur. Please send any updates, corrections or additions to:
Sage Creek Press, PO Box 1373, Silverthorne, Colorado 80498

Keep your book current. To keep the ride information in your guidebook accurate and receive a yearly "update" sheet, mail a self-addressed stamped envelope to:
Sage Creek Press, PO Box 1373, Silverthorne, Colorado 80498

A single track section of Baker's Tank Loop.

Todd Powell

Laura Rossetter biked over 1,500 miles of Summit County's backcountry while revising this guide. In addition to being an avid mountain biker, she is a skilled telemark skier, windsurfer and kayaker. Laura, a teacher and Summit County resident, is the author of *Mountain Biking Colorado's Historic Mining Districts*.

ORDER A COPY OF THIS POPULAR MOUNTAIN BIKE GUIDE
FOR A FRIEND

The Mountain Bike Guide to Summit County, Colorado makes an excellent gift. We will quickly ship your order to you (or directly to your friend). You can request an author autograph to personalize your gift.

Discover sixty-six more Colorado rides with a copy of Laura's other book, *Mountain Biking Colorado's Historic Mining Districts*. To receive additional information about this unique guide or to order a copy, check the appropriate space.

_____(Quantity) *The Mountain Bike Guide to Summit County, Colorado* $9.95 ea.

Colo. only tax   .30 ea.

_____(Quantity) *Mountain Biking Colorado's Historic Mining Districts* $10.95 ea.

Colo. only tax   .33 ea.

_____(Info Only) *Mountain Biking Colorado's Historic Mining Districts*

Postage and handling *per book* $1.75 ea.

Total Enclosed $_____

(Check or money order only)

Please mail the book(s) to this address:

Name: _____

Address: _____

City: _____ State: _____ Zip:_____

Please autograph the book(s): _____

(Name of Recipient)

Mail to: Sage Creek Press, PO Box 1373, Silverthorne, Colorado 80498